KT-379-473

Introduction

The Celts are much less well known to us than the Greeks
and the Romans, although theirs was a great civilization in its
own way. Unlike the Romans, they were not empire-builders,
being very much a tribal society, and so they did not make an
impact in this way.

A major problem for those who seek to know more about
the Celts is the lack of contemporary written history or literature. It is known that they had the ability to write, but they
appear not to have done so. It has been suggested that, perhaps, this was part of their social and religious culture and
that the druids, or priests, had put them under some kind of
taboo not to write things down.

Because of this, theirs was very much an oral tradition. Their
culture is rich in marvellous legends, but these were handed
down by word of mouth and so tend to have several variations, as do many of the Celtic names. It was not until com-
paratively recently that our knowledge of the Celts has been
extended, thanks to archaeology. We have learnt far more about
the lifestyle of the Celts from what has been dug up than from
that which has been written down.

Because they believed that a dead person simply travelled
to the Otherworld, Celtic graves contained not only corpses

but many of the appurtenances that were needed in the mortal world and were though to be needed in the Otherworld. These appurtenances, which include carts, wagons, even horses, as well as dishes, tools and jewellery, have led us to have a greater understanding of the Celts and to appreciate that they were not so primitive as many of us might have believed.

This book, by describing some of the customs as well as some of the legends of the Celts, seeks to add to the reader's knowledge of a people who are still, to a great extent, enveloped in mystery.

Dictionary of
The Celts

ancient worlds

GEDDES &
GROSSET

This edition published 1999 by Geddes & Grosset, an imprint of
Children's Leisure Products Limited

© 1997 Children's Leisure Products Limited,
David Dale House, New Lanark ML11 9DJ, Scotland

Cover image of Celtic chased plaque, 1st century AD,
National Gallery of Wales, courtesy of Werner Forman Archive

All rights reserved. No part of this publication may be
reproduced, stored in a retrieval system, or transmitted,
in any form or by any means, electronic, mechanical,
photocopying, recording or otherwise, without
the prior permission of the copyright holder

ISBN 1 85534 376 2

Printed and bound in the UK

A

AED *see* IBHELL; MONGAN.

AEDA
In Irish Celtic mythology, Aeda was a dwarf at the court of FERGUS MAC LEDA. He was taken by the FILI, EISIRT, to the court of IUBDAN, the king of the diminutive FAYLINN, to prove that there was a race of supposed giants elsewhere.

AED ABRAT
In Irish Celtic mythology, Aed Abrat was the father of FAND and LI BAN.

AFAGDDU
In Welsh Celtic mythology, Afagddu was the son of CERRIDWEN. He was so ugly that his mother sought to give him intellectual skills that would compensate for his unattractive appearance. She thus put together a magic brew that had to be regularly stirred for a year and a day and appointed GWION BACH to stir the potion. Afagddu, however, by strange circumstances was deprived of his promised new skills. *See also* TALIESIN.

AENGHUS *see* OENGHUS.

AICHLEACH
In Irish Celtic mythology, there are various stories relating to the death of FIONN MAC CUMHAILL. According to one of these, he was murdered by Aichleach during a rebellion of the FIANNA.

AIDIN *see* OSCAR.

AILILL
In Irish Celtic mythology, Ailill was the husband of MEDB, queen of Connacht, she being generally held to be the more dominant partner. Ailill's ownership of FINNBHENACH, the white-horned bull of Connacht, although the bull had been born into her herd, made Medb extremely jealous and to compensate for this ownership she sought to acquire DONN CUAILGNE, the great brown bull of Ulster. This was the origin of the TAIN BO CUAILGNE.

AILLEN *see* FIONN MAC CUMHAILL; SAMHAIN.

AINGE *see* GAIBLE.

ALBANACTUS *see* KAMBER; LOCRINUS.

AMHAIRGHIN *or* AMAIRGEN
In Irish Celtic mythology, Amhairghin, whose name exists in various variants, was a warrior and a FILI. He is said to have been a son of MIL and to have been part of the expedition of the Sons of MIL ESPAINE that invaded Ireland. Being a fili, he was considered to have good powers of judgement and was asked by the then inhabitants of Ireland, the

6

TUATHA DE DANANN, to settle a dispute between them and the Sons of Mil Espaine as to who should rule Ireland. Amhairghin suggested that the invaders should set out to sea again to beyond a magical boundary, referred to as the ninth wave, and then attempt the invasion again. The Tuatha tried to stop the Sons of Mil Espaine from landing again but Amhairghin succeeded by some kind of magical means to get the wind to drop and the Sons of Mil Espaine were allowed to land again.

After the Tuatha had been defeated in battle and they had been allotted the underground part of Ireland as their realm and the Sons of Mil Espaine had been allotted the part of Ireland that was above ground as their realm, another problem was posed for Amhairghin. He was asked to intervene in a dispute between EBER FINN and EREMON as to which of them should rule Ireland. He decreed that Eremon should rule first and that on his death Eber Finn should rule. Eber Finn objected to this, and Ireland was divided in two, Eremon ruling the north and Eber Finn ruling the south. This system did not last and war broke out, Eber Finn being killed and Eremon becoming king of the whole of Ireland.

As a fili Amhairghin is credited with several poems.

ANIMALS

In Celtic mythology and beliefs, animals, both domesticated and wild, played a significant part. SHAPE-CHANGING was an intrinsic part of Celtic legend, and the shapes that people or gods adopted or were forced to adopt were those of animals.

7

For example, the nephews of FIONN MAC CUMHAILL were turned into hounds.

STAGS and BOARS were important wild animals in Celtic culture, and HORSES, PIGS, RAMS, BULLS and dogs, especially hunting-hounds, were important domesticated animals.

Archaeological excavations have revealed evidence of animal sacrifice to the various gods.

ANLUAN *see* CET.

ANNW

In Welsh Celtic mythology, Annw was the Otherworld realm ruled over by ARAWN. Arawn features in an early Welsh poem, 'Preiddeu Annw', which describes a journey to Annw to capture a magic CAULDRON. This is thought to have influenced the quest for the Holy GRAIL, prominent in Arthurian legend.

AOBH

In Irish Celtic mythology, Aobh was the daughter of BODB DEARG and the wife of LIR. She bore him four children. On her death, Lir married her sister, AOIFE (1), and she was so jealous of her husband's love for the children of his previous marriage that she turned them into swans for nine hundred years.

AOIFE (1)

In Irish Celtic mythology, Aoife was the sister of AOBH and the second wife of LIR. She was so jealous of Lir's four children by his first marriage that she turned them into swans for nine hundred years. It is said that her father, and the children's grandfather, BODB, was so angry with her for doing this that he turned her into a RAVEN, a bird associated with doom and death. Another legend indicates that she was turned into a crane, which was then killed by MANANNAN MAC LIR and that he used the skin of the crane to make a bag in which to carry his treasures.

AOIFE (2) *or* AIFE

In Irish Celtic mythology, Aoife was the name of the great rival of SCATHACH who taught CUCHULAINN war skills. While studying with Scathach, Cuchulainn defeated Aoife in battle. Later he had an affair with her, the result of the union being a son, CONNLAI.

ARANRHOD

In Welsh Celtic mythology, Aranrhod was the sister of GWYDION FAB DON. When their brother, and possibly Gwydion, had raped GOEWIN, foot-holder to MATH FAB MATHONWY, Gwydion put forward his sister for the post, although she was not a virgin and the post demanded that the holder be a virgin. As she took the test of virginity by stepping over Math's wand, she dropped two bundles. One was DYLAN who leapt into the sea. The other bundle was also a boy, and Gwydion succeeded in picking him up and concealing him. He became LLEU LLAW GYFFES.

ARAWN

In Welsh Celtic mythology, Arawn was the king of ANNW, the Welsh Otherworld. He is best known in legend for his association with Pwyll, lord of Dyfed. One day when Pwyll was out hunting he saw a strange pack of hounds, seemingly without an owner, overcoming a stag. He chased off the hounds and set his own hounds to the stag. Arawn then appeared and told Pwyll that he had done him a great insult by chasing off his hounds and that he would have to be recompensed in some way. It was agreed that to make up for the insult Pwyll would try to kill Hafgan, Arawn's deadly rival, with whom he is said to have had an annual contest. In order to do this, Pwyll was to assume the shape of Arawn and go to live in Annw for a year while Arawn was to take on the form of Pwyll and go to rule Dyfed for a year.

ARBETH

In Welsh Celtic mythology, Arbeth was the chief court of Pwyll.

ARGOED LLWYFAIN *see* Urien.

ARTHUR

Arthur was associated with Celtic mythology, although he was a historical figure from around the fifth or early sixth centuries, after the Romans left Britain in the period that is known as the Dark Ages. In the Arthurian saga, centred on the adventures of the Knights of the Round Table, Arthur is a medieval king. There appear to be no contemporary Celtic references to Arthur, either as a historical or as a legendary figure, although he did become involved in the story of Culhwch and in the story of the journey to Annw to acquire the enchanted cauldron. Arthur is associated with Celtic myth but this may have been a postdated association.

It is likely that he came to power in the dying days of the Celts and that the stories surrounding him grew as they were driven farther and farther from their native land. Certainly there seems to be little, if any, evidence to link Arthur to the Celtic period.

B

BADB

In Irish Celtic mythology, Badb was an Irish war-goddess. She is depicted both as a single goddess and as one aspect of a triple goddess, the other two aspects being NEMAIN and MACHA. She is depicted as having the form of a RAVEN or a hooded crow, and her name indicates 'rage' or 'violence'. The war-goddesses could strike terror into the hearts of armies, as, even if they did not take an active part in a battle, they were often present. Badb was said to be able to select those who would die in battle and was thought to be able to alter the course of a battle to suit her own desires. Before a battle she was supposedly to be found beside a stream engaged in washing the armour and weapons of those who were destined to die.

BALOR OF THE EVIL EYE

In Irish Celtic mythology, Balor of the Evil Eye was the king of the FOMORII. A GIANT and monster with one eye, he was greatly feared. It was said that the eyelid over his one eye was so huge and heavy that it had to be levered open by several men. When it was open it was a source of destruction since it could kill anyone, including whole armies, that Balor looked upon.

Since it had been forecast that Balor would be killed by his own grandson, he was at pains to make sure that no man got near his daughter, ETHLINN, whom he locked away in the GLASS TOWER on TORY ISLAND or possibly in a cave. CIAN, helped by a druidess, succeeded in gaining entrance to where Ethlinn was and seduced her. The story varies as to whether she had one child by him or triplets. The legend that indicates triplets tells how Balor threw the babies in the sea, only one escaping. In either event, Ethlinn had a surviving son by Cian, and in time the prophecy concerning Balor's grandson came true. The child was LUGH, and it was he who killed Balor by putting out his one eye with his slingshot. He drove it right through the back of his head and killed many of the Fomorii as well. Balor's corpse is then said to have been hung on a sacred hazel tree where it dripped poison and split in two.

BANBHA *or* **BANB** *see* ERIU; MAC CUILL.

BANSHEE *see* BEAN SIDHE.

BEANN GHULBAN
In Irish Celtic mythology, Beann Ghulban was a monstrous BOAR without ears or a tail that originally had been born as a human child to the wife of DONN. It was so named from the area where it roamed. It was placed under a bond by its father, ROC, to kill DIARMAID ua Duibhne, and duly did this when Diarmaid was out hunting with FIONN.

BEAN SIDHE
In Irish Celtic mythology, Bean Sidhe was a female fairy or

13

spirit that became attached to a particular family. Known in English as banshee, it was said that she would set up an eerie wail when a member of the family was going to die.

BEBO
In Irish Celtic mythology, Bebo was the wife of IUBDAN and so the queen of FAYLINN. She went with her husband to Ulster to visit what to the diminutive people of Faylinn was a race of GIANTS, Iubdan having been put under a *geis* or bond by EISIRT to go there. They were held captive there.

BEDWYR *see* YSPADDADEN.

BELENUS *or* BELENOS *or* BEL
In Gaulish Celtic mythology, Belenus was a god who was associated with light, the word *bel* meaning 'bright'. He was also associated with the sun and with healing and later became linked with the classical god Apollo.

BELI
In Welsh Celtic mythology, Beli was the father of LLUDD and LLEFELYS. He is also said to have been the husband of DON.

BELTANE *or* BELTAINE *or* BELTENE
One of the four great annual Celtic festivals was Beltane. It was celebrated on 1 May and marked the beginning of the Celtic summer. It was named after BELENUS and was associated with bonfires lit the night before the festival. The ordinary household fires would be extinguished and the DRUIDS would light bonfires, supposedly using torches lit by the rays

of the sun. The festival was associated with regeneration and regrowth after the ravages of winter.

BENDIGEID VRAN *or* BENDIGEIDFRAN

In Welsh Celtic mythology, Bendigeid Vran, popularly known as Bran the Blessed, was the son of LLYR, the brother of BRANWEN and MANAWYDAN, and the half-brother of EFNISIEN and NISIEN. He is best known for the expedition that he led to Ireland to rescue his sister Branwen from her husband, the Irish king, MATHOLWCH. Bendigeid Vran had agreed to Branwen's marriage to the Irish king, but when Matholwch was at the court of Bendigeid to escort Branwen back to Ireland, Efnisien, who was noted for his mischief, mutilated the horses of Matholwch, an act that the Irish king took as a great insult.

Matholwch went back to Ireland, taking with him a magic CAULDRON that Bendigeid Vran had given him, either as a wedding gift or as compensation for the action of Efnisien. The cauldron could restore the wounded to health and the dead to life.

When Matholwch reached Ireland, still mindful of Efnisien's insult, he began to ill-treat Branwen. When this news reached his ears, her brother decided to invade Ireland to rescue Branwen and to teach Matholwch a lesson. At first some attempt was made to establish peace, and the son of Branwen and Matholwch, GWERN, was to take over the sovereignty of Ireland. Unfortunately, Efnisien's love of malice and mischief came to the fore again, and he threw the boy in a blazing fire.

There was a terrible battle that, at first, Matholwch's men were winning because of their possession of the magic healing cauldron. Efnisien succeeded in destroying this, and Bendigeid's forces began to win. Both sides suffered terrible losses. According to legend, of the Irish only five pregnant women were left alive because they had hidden in a cave, and to them fell the task of repopulating the country. Bendigeid was mortally wounded and, as he lay dying, asked his followers to decapitate him and to take his head back home and bury it in the WHITE MOUNT in London. The Celts believed that the soul lay in the head and that it therefore could go on living without the body. Thus Bendigeid's head is said to have gone on talking, and even eating, for the very long time that it took the survivors, seven in number, including PRYDERI and TALIESIN, to get to London.

Branwen was so grief-stricken at all the bloodshed that she had inadvertently caused that she died of a broken heart and was buried in the Isle of Anglesey.

BHUILG *see* FIR BHOLG.

BITH
In Irish Celtic mythology, Bith was a son of Noah and the father of CESAIR. With FINTAN and LADRA, he was one of the three men who took part in her invasion of Ireland.

BLATHNAD *see* CUCHULAINN.

BLEDDYN
In Welsh Celtic mythology, Bleddyn was the son of the brothers GWYDION FAB DON and GILFAETHWAY and the brother of HYDWYN and HWYCHDWN. He was born in the third year of

Gwydion's and Gilfaethwy's punishment so was born in the shape of a wolf.

BLODEUWEDD

In Welsh Celtic mythology, Blodeuwedd was a beautiful maiden whose name translates as 'flower face'. She was created out of oak, broom and meadowsweet by GWYDION and MATH to be the bride of LLEU LLAW GYFFES to circumvent the curse that was put on him by his mother, ARANRHOD, that he should never marry a mortal woman until she herself found him one, which she had no intention of doing.

Blodeuwedd was unfaithful to Lleu with GRONW PEBYR, and they planned to murder Lleu, but he could be killed only under certain strange conditions. She found out from Lleu what these conditions were, in particular what stance he had to adopt before he could be killed. Gronw tried to kill Lleu with a spear but succeeded only in wounding him, and Gronw was killed by him. Blodeuwedd was turned into an owl and became an outcast.

BOANN

In Irish Celtic mythology, Boann was the mother of OENGHUS by the DAGHDA. At that time she was the wife of ELCMAR, and the Daghda had tricked him into going away while he had sexual relations with his wife. The Daghda succeeded in causing nine months to seem like a day, and so when Elcmar returned he thought that his trip had lasted only one day instead of nine months. Oenghus was brought up by MIDHIR.

Another legend has it that Boann was the wife of Nechtan

and the sister of Elcmar. She was said to be a water-goddess and to have given her name to the River Boyne.

BOAR

In Celtic mythology and culture, the boar was important. Boars were admired for their ferocity and were associated with war. Helmets used in war were often adorned with crests in the shape of boars, and war trumpets with boar heads were common. The boar motif is often presented with the dorsal bristles raised, indicating that it is in attacking mood.

Like the STAG, the boar was used as a symbol of hunting and it was also associated with feasting

Pork was popular for feasts, particularly with the Irish Celts, both in the mortal world and the OTHERWORLD.

Boars also played a part in Celtic legend. One of the most famous of the legendary boars was the foster brother of DIARMAID ua Duibhne. ROC had a son by the wife of DONN as a result of an illicit affair. Donn was furious and crushed the child to death. Roc brought the child back to life, but it came back to life in the shape of a monstrous boar without ears or tail. The boar was placed under a *geis* or bond by Roc to kill Donn's son, Diarmaid. The monstrous boar was known as BEANN GHULBAN from the area where it roamed. When Diarmaid and FIONN were out hunting, the boar fulfilled its bond by mortally wounding Diarmaid. Fionn, who could have saved him with water from his healing hands, chose not to because Diarmaid had gone off with GRAINNE, who was to have been married to Fionn.

BODB DEARG

In Irish Celtic mythology, Bodb Dearg is said by some sources to have been the son of the DAGHDA and to have succeeded him as father of the gods. According to one source, he was the father of AOBH, but other sources indicate that she was his foster daughter. He is said to have identified the dream woman of OENGHUS as CAER and took him to her. On alternate years she became a swan and Oenghus himself turned into a swan and flew away with her.

BOGS

In Celtic mythology and culture, bogs were important. Votive offerings to the gods were often deposited in bogs. Perhaps it was thought that bogs, which are treacherous in that the ground above them can appear quite firm although underneath they are swampy and dangerous, contained spirits that had to be appeased. CAULDRONS were often deposited in bogs, and a particularly fine example of this is the GUNDESTRUP CAULDRON, and parts of wagons and carts have also been retrieved from bogs. Bogs also seem to have been used for animal and human sacrifice, as remains of animals and humans have been uncovered from them. *See* LINDOW MAN.

BOUDICCA *or* BOADICEA

In British history, Boudicca was a warrior queen. She was the wife of PRASUTAGAS, the leader of the ICENI tribe. Her husband had succeeded in retaining some degree of autonomy from the Romans, but when he died the Romans plundered the royal goods, raped the daughters of Prasutagas and Boudicca, and flogged Boudicca. Boudicca then raised a spirited campaign against the Romans and met with some success until she was eventually defeated in battle. She is said to have taken poison after the defeat.

BRAN (1)

In Irish Celtic mythology, Bran was the son of Febal and was lured away to the OTHERWORLD by the vision of a beautiful woman. He set out to find her, taking with him his three foster brothers and twenty-seven warriors. After various adventures, Bran and his companions met MANANNAN MAC LIR, the god of the sea, on his chariot, who is said to have changed the sea into a flowery plain and then changed it back again. They then came to the Otherworld realm known as TIR NA MBAN, the Land of the Women. Legend has it that one of the women who lived there threw a ball of string out to Bran. It stuck to his hand and so the ship was hauled out of the sea to land on the magic island.

Bran and his followers stayed for a while in the Land of the Women, enjoying a comfortable life surrounded by beautiful women, but some of the men became restless and wanted to return home to Ireland. According to one source, they were warned against so doing by one of the women, who told them that, although they felt that they had been with the women for only one year, they had actually been there for many hundreds of years. She is said to have further warned them that they would fall to dust as soon as they set foot on land, as they would have far outlived the usual age span. Either they chose to ignore this warning, or the warning was never given.

In any event, they set sail for Ireland. One of the party leapt from the ship on to the Irish shore and instantly became a heap of dust. Bran is said to have called out to some people on the shore to tell them of his adventures and then to have sailed off, never to be seen again.

BRAN (2)
In Irish Celtic mythology, Bran was also the name of one of the sons of Tuireann, who was born to her when she had been turned into a wolfhound by the mistress of her husband, Illan. Both Bran and his brother, Sgeolan, were born as wolfhounds and became the faithful hounds of Fionn mac Cumhaill.

BRANDUBH *see* Mongan.

BRAN THE BLESSED
In Welsh Celtic mythology, a name popularly given to Bendigeid Vran.

BRANWEN
In Welsh Celtic mythology, Branwen was the sister of Bendigeid Vran and wife of Matholwch. It was Matholwch's ill-treatment of her that led to Bendigeid's invasion of Ireland and to his death and the destruction of most of his followers. *See also* Efnisien.

BREASAL
In Irish Celtic mythology, Breasal was the king of Hy-Breasal.

BREGON *see* Mil.

BRES

In Irish Celtic mythology, there was more than one person called Bres, and they tend to become confused. The best-known one is the Bres who took over from NUADA when he lost an arm in battle and had to abdicate as king of the TUATHA DE DANANN. Bres was part FOMORII on his father's side, his father being ELATHA, and part Tuatha De Danann on his mother's side, his mother, Eri, having had an affair with Elatha. Bres was a bad and tyrannical ruler. He was forced to abdicate in favour of Nuada, who had had a silver arm fitted by DIAN CECHT, and defected to the Fomorii. This led to the second Battle of MAGH TUIREDH. He was captured in the battle but was released by the Tuatha on condition that he gave them advice on agriculture.

BRIAN *see* IUCHAR.

BRICRIU

In Irish Celtic mythology, Bricriu was an Ulster champion who was famous for his malice and love of mischief in the way that the Welsh EFNISIEN was. He is said to have given a feast for the men of Ulster and the men of Connacht. There was much competition to carve the meat at such a feast, as this honour traditionally went to the most notable warrior present. In order to cause trouble, Bricriu secretly persuaded three of the notable warriors all to claim this honour, the three warriors being CUCHULAINN, CONALL CERNACH and Laoghaire Buadhach. The three were sent to MEDB to have their claim judged, and she judged in favour of Cuchulainn, but the other two refused to accept the decision. They were then all three sent to Cu Roi mac Dairi, the king of Munster. He also decided in favour of Cuchulainn.

Legend also has it that Bricriu was asked to judge the contest between Donn Cuailgne and Finnbhenach, but he was trampled to death by the two fighting bulls.

BRIGID *or* BRIGIT

In Irish Celtic mythology, Brigid seems to have been one of the goddesses who was both a single goddess and a triple goddess. Her name meant 'exalted one', and she was associated with healing, fertility, crafts, poetry and learning. According to one legend, she was the daughter of the Daghda and may have been the wife of Bres.

As well as being a pagan goddess, Brigid became a Christian saint who took over some of the traditions and associations of the goddess as well as her name.

BRI LEITH *see* Midhir.

BRUTUS

In Romano-British Celtic mythology, Brutus is said to have been the founder of the British people. The great-grandson of the Trojan Aeneas, he is supposed to have landed at Totnes in Devon and to have subjugated the giants who then inhabited the country.

BULL

In Celtic mythology and culture, the bull was important. It

was a symbol of strength and virility as well as aggression, the latter symbolized by its horns, which were often depicted in carvings, figurines, etc, in exaggerated form. Bull heads were sometimes used as handles for buckets, and bull statuettes seem to have existed from the seventh century BC.

Bull sacrifice appears to have been common among the Celts, and examples are depicted on the silver GUNDESTRUP CAULDRON. The bull was also associated with other Celtic rituals. At the TARBHFEIS, which took place to chose a high king of Ireland, a bull was slain and its flesh eaten and its blood drunk by a DRUID, who then went to sleep and was supposed to dream of the person who was to be high king.

In mythology, the most famous legend involving a bull is contained in the TAIN BO CUAILGNE, the story of how DONN CUAILGNE, the famous great brown bull of Ulster, was taken by MEDB of Connacht.

C

CAER

In Irish Celtic mythology, CAER was the daughter of ETHAL ANUBAL. OENGHUS had a dream about a beautiful maiden and fell in love with her. He determined to find her and sought the help of BODB DEARG. He was able to identify the girl as Caer. Oenghus asked MEDB of Connacht to intervene with Ethal to get him to let Oenghus marry his daughter. Ethal, however, said that in alternate years Caer turned into a swan and directed him to a lake where he would find her swimming with one hundred and fifty other swans on the Feast of Samhain. If Oenghus was able to identify Caer among all the other swans and she wanted to go with him, then Oenghus could have her. Oenghus was able to identify Caer, and he turned into a swan and flew off with her.

CAER LOYW *see* MABON.

CAIRBRE

In Irish Celtic mythology, there are several people called Cairbre, but the best known is the son of CORMAC MAC AIRT and a king of Ireland. He went to war with the FIANNA after he had refused to pay a tribute to them and destroyed them at

GABHRA. He killed OSCAR in single combat but was himself mortally wounded.

CALADIN *see* CUCHULAINN.

CALATIN
In Irish Celtic mythology, Calatin and his twenty-seven sons were killed by CUCHULAINN. His wife bore him six monstrous children posthumously, and MEDB looked after them while they learned magic skills so that they could help her defeat Cuchulainn. They later used their magic art against Cuchulainn and marched with Erc against him in the battle that led to his death.

CANO
An historical figure who is said to have died around 688, Cano is also a subject of legend, although it may have its basis in some fact. It is said that he was the son of a Scottish king and that he was exiled to Ireland. There he met an elderly man called Marcan who had a very beautiful young wife of the name of Cred. She fell in love with Cano and at a feast drugged the entire company apart from him. She then asked him to make her his mistress. He, conscious of the laws of hospitality and his duty to his host, refused but pledged his undying love and gave her a stone that he said contained his life. Cano was recalled to Scotland on his father's death, and he became king. According to legend, each year he and Cred tried to meet in Ireland but were always frustrated in their attempts by Cred's jealous stepson, Colcu. One year they decided to meet at Lough Crede. Colcu is said to have intercepted Cano

and driven him off. Not realizing this, Cred assumed that Cano was not going to turn up and jumped from her horse and dashed her brains out against a rock. As she fell, she dropped the precious stone that was said to contain the life of Cano. It smashed into several pieces, and he died three days later.

CARATACUS
The chief of a British Celtic tribe called the Catuvellauni was CARATACUS. He led a campaign against the Roman invaders but he was handed over to his Roman enemies by Cartimandua, the queen of the Brigantes. He is said to have been taken to Rome, where he was pardoned by the emperor Claudius.

CARADAWC
In Welsh Celtic mythology, Caradawc was a son of BENDIGEID VRAN. When his father set out for Ireland to challenge MATHOLWCH for his treatment of BRANWEN, he left Caradawc with six companions in charge of his kingdom. When news of Bendigeid Vran's death reached his kingdom, Caswallan ousted Caradawc and took over. Caradawc and his companions were killed by Caswallan.

CARRIDWEN *see* CERRIDWEN.

CARTIMANDUA
The queen of the Brigantes tribe who is said to have handed CARATACUS over to the Romans was Cartimandua.

CASWALLAN *see* CARADAWC.

27

CATHBAD *or* CATHBHADH

In Irish Celtic mythology, Cathbad, whose name has various variant spellings, was a DRUID at the court of CONCHOBAR MAC NESSA. He is said to have been the father of DEICHTIRE and so the grandfather of CUCHULAINN. It was Cathbad who is said to have forecast that DEIRDRE would be very beautiful but that she would bring grief and destruction to Ireland.

CAULDRON

A recurrent theme in Celtic mythology is the cauldron. The DAGHDA had an inexhaustible cauldron from which no one went away hungry. BENDIGEID VRAN gave MATHOLWCH a magic cauldron that could heal the wounded and revive the dead. MIDHIR also owned a magic cauldron. Evidence has been uncovered on several archaeological sites of cauldrons. The Celts had a habit of preserving cauldrons by burying them in lakes and bogs, often as votive offerings to the gods. Of these the most famous is the splendid GUNDESTRUP CAULDRON.

CELTCHAR *see* NIAMH.

CELTIC LANGUAGE

The Celtic languages formed a group that was a branch of the Indo-European family of languages. They are sometimes divided into *Continental Celtic*, now extinct languages spoken from about 500 BC to AD 500 from the Black Sea to Iberia, and *Insular Celtic*, which is usually further divided into *Brythonic* or *British Celtic* and *Goidelic* or *Irish Celtic*. Goidelic Celtic is often referred to by philologists as *Q-Celtic* and Brythonic Celtic as *P-Celtic* because of a sound change that took place from *q* to *p* in the Brythonic languages. Compare, for example, Irish *ceann* with Welsh *pen*, both meaning 'head'. It is believed these two linguistic groups began to go their separate ways around two and a half thousand years ago. Goidelic Celtic is the source of Irish and Scottish Gaelic and also the source of the now little used Manx Gaelic.

CELTS

The Celts were first recorded by the Greeks as *KELTOI*, deriving perhaps from a native word meaning 'hidden people'. This association with concealment may have come from the fact that, although writing was known to them and, indeed, was used, for example, on gravestones and pottery from early times, they did not commit any of their history or legends to writing until about the sixth century AD. The Celts are thought to have been under some form of prohibition by their DRUIDS not to commit things to writing, writing being a kind of taboo.

It is thought that they originated in central Europe, in the basin of the Danube, the Alps and parts of France and Germany around 1200 BC. They were originally farmers but became pioneers of iron-working. Around the sixth century BC they are thought to have spread into Spain and Portugal. Over the next few hundred years they spread into Britain, northern Italy, Greece and the Balkans. Unlike the Romans, the Celts never formed an empire, being essentially a tribal people. In the first century BC they were defeated by the Romans and by Germanic tribes and were virtually confined to Ireland, England and Wales. The Roman invasion of Britain in AD 43 further depleted them, and the arrival of the Anglo-Saxons in the fifth century pushed them into the far corners of Britain. Thus, in time, the Celtic civilization was destroyed by the Romans and by the expansion of the Germanic tribes. It survived most energetically in Ireland, which was not invaded by the Romans. *See also* HALLSTATT; LA TÈNE.

CENN CRUIACH *see* TIGERNMAS.

CERRIDWEN *or* **CARRIDWEN**
In Welsh Celtic mythology, Cerridwen was the mother of a very ugly son, AFAGDDU, and a very beautiful daughter, Crearwy. To compensate Afaggdu for his extremely unattractive features, Cerridwen set out to give him the gifts of wisdom, inspiration and universal knowledge. In order to achieve this, she made a potion of various herbs and put the potion to brew in a CAULDRON. She selected GWION BACH to stir the potion for a year and a day, after which time three drops of the fluid would have the desired effect on Afagddu. She also selected a blind man, Morda, to stoke the fire on which the cauldron was bubbling.

Unfortunately for Cerridwen and Afagddu, there was a hitch in her plans. As Gwion was faithfully stirring the potion towards the end of the allotted time, three drops of the hot liquid splashed on his finger and he put it in his mouth to cool it. By this action he got the benefit of the magical potion that was intended for Afagddu and became full of wisdom and knowledge. The cauldron, having given up its knowledge-giving essence, split in two and spilt its now poisonous substance on the surrounding floor.

Gwion was terrified and fled the scene. Cerridwen flew into a rage when she discovered that her son had been deprived of his intended wisdom and knowledge, and gave chase to Gwion, having beaten Morda. She turned herself into a terrible black hag and was catching up with the boy when he turned into a hare in order to run faster and get away from her. The whole chase then became a series of SHAPE-CHANGING. Cerridwen turned into a greyhound in order to overtake the hare. At this, Gwion took to the water as a salmon, and Cerridwen counteracted by becoming an otter. Gwion then tried the air instead of water and transformed himself into a bird, but Cerridwen turned herself into a hawk. In desperation, Gwion dropped down on to the threshing floor of a barn and turned himself into a grain of corn, thinking that he would be safe among the many thousands of other grains. However, the wily Cerridwen turned herself into a hen and succeeded in locating the grain of corn that was Gwion. She swallowed him, presumably thinking that that was the end of him.

However, Cerridwen was not as successful as she thought she had been. When she resumed her usual human form, she discovered that she was pregnant. Nine months later she gave birth to a boy who was the reincarnation of Gwion and extremely beautiful. She did not want to keep the boy, but she did not really want to be kill him, so she put him in a leather bag and threw it in the river. The bag ended up in the fish weir belonging to the father of ELFFIN, and it was Elffin who found it. On taking the baby boy out of the bag, he is said to have commented on the beauty of the baby, particularly on his 'radiant brow'. Thus the baby boy got the name of TALIESIN.

Cerridwen, as befits her role in the story, is said to have been the keeper of the cauldron in the OTHERWORLD, the cauldron in which inspiration and knowledge were brewed. She was associated with the sow, a symbol of fecundity.

CERNUNNOS

In Celtic mythology and culture, Cernunnos was a lord of the animals. His name means 'the horned one'. He is usually depicted as wearing horns or antlers, sometimes decorated with a TORC, and often has both human and animal ears. He is often shown as sitting in a cross-legged position, is often accompanied by a STAG or BULL and is frequently presented as holding a RAM-headed serpent. He was probably associated with fertility, abundance and regeneration as well as with hunting. Cernunnos survived into the Roman-Celtic period.

CESAIR

In Irish Celtic mythology, Cesair was the granddaughter of Noah and daughter of Bith, who led the first invaders to Ireland before the Flood, a group consisting of fifty women and three men, Bith, LADRA and FINTAN. Cesair became the wife of Fintan. Her journey features in the LEABHAR GABHALA EIREANN.

CET

In Irish Celtic mythology, Cet was a warrior of Connacht who, with his brother Anluan, was invited by MEDB to take part in the quest for the DONN CUAILGNE. They were also asked to take part in a feast before the quest, and Cet claimed the privilege of carving the roast meat, a role that traditionally went to the greatest warrior present. However, CONALL CERNACH arrived and claimed the honour for himself. Cet reluctantly agreed but taunted Conall that if his brother Anluan had been present, Conall would have had to yield the honour to him. At that point Conall removed the bloody head of Anluan from a pouch and threw it on the table, showing that he had already defeated Anluan.

Cet, according to some sources, stole a 'brain-ball' from CON-CHOBAR's court at EMHAIN MACHA and later used it in a slingshot to strike Conchobar on the forehead.

CHARIOTS

Of great importance to the Celts were chariots, especially for use in war. They were also important as religious transport, with goddesses often being depicted as riding on them. An indication of how important chariots and carts were to the Celts is the fact that the elite of Celtic society were often buried with their chariots, carts or wagons. This is evident in the HALLSTATT PERIOD.

CIAN

In Irish Celtic mythology, Cian was the son of DIAN CECHT, the god of medicine. He had a cow, which was stolen by BALOR, and he went to retrieve it from the island of TORY. While he was there he found his way into the GLASS TOWER in which

Balor had imprisoned his daughter ETHLINN so that no man could get near her. He was trying to avert a prophecy that he, Balor, would be killed by his own grandson. Cian is said to have seduced Ethlinn, who bore him a son called LUGH who did indeed kill Balor.

CIARAN, ST *see* ISLAY.

CIGFA
In Welsh Celtic mythology, Cigfa was the wife of PRYDERI. She and Pryderi had various adventures along with MANAWYDAN and RHIANNON.

CIL COED *see* LLWYD.

CILYDD
In Welsh Celtic mythology, Cilydd was the husband of GOLEUD-DYDD and father of CULHWCH.

CIRCLE
In Celtic culture, the circle motif, particularly the concentric circle, was important. It may, like the WHEEL, have been associated with the SUN, and it may also have been a symbol of eternity.

COBTHACH *see* UGAINE MOR.

COBTHACH COEL
In Irish Celtic mythology, Cobthach Coel drove LABHRAIDH LOINGSECH into exile and was the cause of him losing his voice.

COCHAR CRUFE *see* UATHACH.

COEL *see* HELENA.

COLCHU *see* CANO.

COLUMBA, ST *or* **COLUMCILLE** *see* IONA; ISLAY.

CONAIRE MOR
In Irish Celtic mythology, Conaire Mor was, according to some
sources, the son of EOCHAIDH AIREMH and his own daughter—
for details of how this came to be, *see* MIDHIR. Various bonds
were placed upon him at his birth, but he chose to ignore them.
In particular he ignored warnings not to go to DA DERGA'S
HOSTEL and he met his death there.

CONALL CERNACH *or* **CEARNACH**
In Irish Celtic legend, there are several people called Conall
and they tend to become confused with each other. Of these,
Conall Cernach, also known as Conall of the Victories, is
the best known. He was one of the three warriors who
vied for the honour of carving the roast meat at the feast of
BRICRIU.

It was he who killed Mesgedra, king of Leinster, and made
a 'brain-ball' of his brains and lime. This was given to
CONCHOBAR, who kept it as a treasure. It was later stolen by
CET, who used it in a slingshot and struck Conchobar's forehead, although some sources attribute this to Conall
Cernach. It was not the immediate cause of Conchobar's
death but it is supposed to have led to it.

Conall Cernach is sometimes confused with CONNLAI, also
sometimes known as Conall, who was the child of
CUCHULAINN by AOIFE (2). When Connlai went to Ireland, he

was challenged to fight by Conall Cernach and was defeated
and killed by him.

CONAN MAC FEBAR *see* GLASS TOWER.

CONAN'S TOWER *see* GLASS TOWER.

CONARAN *see* IRNAN.

CONCHOBAR MAC NESSA
In Irish Celtic mythology, Conchobar mac Nessa was the son
of NESSA. She was the wife of the giant FACHTNA, but, according to one legend, Fachtna might not have been
Conchobar's father. Instead, he might have been the natural
son of the druid CATHBAD.

Conchobar became king of Ulster when Nessa would
agree either to marry FERGUS MAC ROTH or have an affair
with him only if he would agree to her son becoming king
for a year in his place. At the end of the year, Conchobar refused to give up the throne and Fergus went into exile.
Conchobar had at his court of EMHAIN MACHA, a group of
highly trained warriors, the RED BRANCH.

Another well-known legend concerning Conchobar relates
to DEIRDRE. She was the daughter of his FILI, and it was
prophesied that she would become the most beautiful
woman in Ireland but that she would bring great grief and
destruction to the country. Hearing of these forecasts,
many people wanted to spare Ireland the prophesied suffering and advocated killing Deirdre at birth. However,
Conchobar was intrigued by the prophecy relating to her
great beauty and refused to have the baby girl killed, saying

that he would marry her when she came of age. When Deirdre came of age, however, Conchobar was quite an old man and she did not relish marrying him. Instead she fell in love with NAOISE and persuaded him to elope with her to Alba, or Scotland.

Conchobar was absolutely furious at their elopement, but, after a few years, he pretended to forgive them and offered them an amnesty if they would go back to Ireland. He sent Fergus mac Roth and some companions to ask them to return and guaranteed their safety. Conchobar, however, went back on his word and had Naoise and his brothers, who had gone with Naoise and Deirdre when they eloped, put to death. Fergus was very angry with Conchobar for breaking his word, attacked Conchobar's court, killed many Ulstermen and defected to MEDB of Connacht, the bitter enemy of Conchobar. Meanwhile, Deirdre flung herself from a moving chariot and dashed her brains out.

Another legend about Conchobar concerns his death. CONALL CERNACH had killed Mesgedra, king of Leinster, and had removed the dead king's brain to make a 'brain-ball' out of it by mashing the brain up and mixing it with lime. A brain-ball was said to be a particularly deadly missile if it was flung at someone. It was regarded as a treasure by Conchobar, but it was stolen secretly from him by CET. Some time later, Cet, although some say it was Conall Cernach, used it in battle as ammunition in a slingshot and hit Conchobar on the forehead. Conchobar's doctors told him that he would die if they removed the brain-ball, which had penetrated his head, but that he would be all right if he simply remained calm and never lost his temper. In time, Conchobar failed to obey this instruction. He lost his temper, the brain-ball split open inside his head and he was killed.

CONGANCHAS MAC DAINE *see* NIAMH.

CONNACHT
In Irish Celtic legend, Connacht was one of the five provinces into which the FIR BHOLG divided Ireland. Traditionally it was the great rival and enemy of ULSTER. MEDB of Connacht fought a war against Ulster to acquire DONN CUAILNGE, the great brown bull of Ulster. *See also* TAIN BO CUAILGNE.

CONNLAI
In Irish Celtic mythology, Connlai, sometimes known as Conall, possibly from confusion with CONALL CERNACH, was the son of CUCHULAINN and AOIFE (2), the great rival of SCATHACH, from whom Cuculainn learnt the arts of war. Having defeated Aoife, who was a great warrior and sorcerer, he then had a child by her.

The boy remained behind with Scathach and learnt the arts of war from her after his father returned to Ireland. He grew up to be a great warrior and eventually went to Ireland, being told before he set sail that he must on no account reveal his identity to anyone who challenged him. The people of Ireland, hearing of his great deeds, are supposed to have sent a champion to meet him as his boat approached the Irish shore. The champion chosen was Conall Cernach, but he was defeated and killed by Connlai.

Next Cuchulainn himself challenged Connlai, especially when Connlai refused to reveal his name or identity. It is said that EMER, wife of Cuchulainn, warned him that this new mighty warrior could only be his own son, but he refused to listen. The two fought a bitter battle that Cuchulainn won in the end. As Connlai lay dying, he at last revealed his identity, and Cuchulainn was filled with remorse and grief.

CORANAID

In Welsh Celtic mythology, the Coranaid were a group of small people who could overhear everything, no matter how low it was whispered. They were one of three plagues that disturbed the reign of LLUDD. Lludd and his brother LLEFELYS devised a plan by which they fed everyone large numbers of a new kind of insect. Everyone else was either unharmed or simply felt some discomfort but the insects poisoned the Coranaids.

CORMAC CAS *see* SAMHAIR.

CORMAC MAC AIRT

In Irish Celtic mythology, Cormac mac Airt appears in various stories, although he is also supposed to have been a historic king around the middle of the second century. He is said to have been the father of CAIRBRE and of GRAINNE. Legend has it that he was lured to visit the OTHERWORLD by MANANNAN MAC LIR. The latter appeared in disguise and offered the king three magic wishes in exchange for a bough of three golden apples that produced a healing music when they were shaken. When Manannan claimed his three wishes, he abducted Cormac's wife and children. Cormac went off in pursuit of them, was surrounded by a mysterious thick mist and found himself in the Otherworld and had his wife and children restored to him. Cormac was given a golden cup by Manannan. It would split in three if three lies were told over it but it would be made whole again if three truths were told. When Cormac died the cup is said to have disappeared.

CRAFTINY
In Irish Celtic mythology, Craftiny was the harper whose magic HARP revived the powers of speech of LABHRAIDH LOINGSECH.

CREARWY *see* CERRIDWEN; TALIESIN.

CRED *see* CANO.

CREIDDYLAD *see* GWYN AP NUDD; LLUD LLAW EREINT.

CREIDHNE *see* GOIBHNIU; LUCHTA.

CRUNDCHU *or* **CRUNNCHU** *see* MACHA.

CUCHULAINN
In Irish Celtic mythology, Cuchulainn is the epitome of the warrior hero. There are many legends about him, and sometimes these become confused. He is said to be the son of DEICHTIRE but probably not by her husband, SUALTAM. Instead

he may have been the son of LUGH, although some say that CONCHOBAR MAC NESSA was his father. He was not originally named Cuchulainn since his mother gave him the name of SETANTA. While he still went under that name and was still a youth, he is said to have successfully undertaken his first heroic feat by single-handedly defeating fifty young men in the service of Conchobar at EMHAIN MACHA.

Later, also while he was still a youth, he was attacked by the hound of Cullan, a SMITH, a hound that was renowned for its ferocity. Setanta is said to have thrown a ball at the animal's gaping jaws so that it swallowed it. He then seized the dog and dashed its brains out against a rock. Cullan was not at all happy about the loss of his dog and complained bitterly. Setanta then offered to fulfil the role of guard dog to Cullan as long as he needed one. By this means did he come by the name by which he is better known, Cuchulainn, the Hound of Cullan. He then became inextricably associated with dogs and hounds and was put under a *geis* or bond never to eat dog flesh or this would bring about his ruin.

He was then given the choice of having either long life or fame, and he chose fame. One of his first acts of heroism was to do battle with the three monstrous sons of NECHTA SCENE. He defeated them, decapitated them, as was the habit of Celtic warriors, and hung their heads from his chariot. Cuchulainn is said to have had several important companions to aid him in his acts of bravery. One of these was his charioteer, LAEG, another was GAE-BHOLG, his magic spear, and another was his sword, Caladin.

Legend has it that Cuchulainn wanted to take EMER for his wife, but he felt that he had to prove his worth before he sought her hand. Thus it was that he left Ireland and went to the home of SCATHACH, the female warrior and prophetess, to learn the skills of war. While there, he defeated AOIFE (2), Scathach's great rival. He made her his mistress and she bore him a son, CONNLAI. When Cuchulainn returned to Ireland, Connlai stayed behind and was taught by Scathach to be a great warrior like his father. In time Connlai wanted to go to Ireland to find his father, but Scathach made him promise never to reveal his name or identity while he was in Ireland, no matter who asked. Connlai was challenged by CONALL CERNACH, whom he defeated and killed. The youth was then challenged by the great Cuchulainn himself, although Emer, now his wife, is said to have warned him of the likely identity of the young champion. Cuchulainn ignored her warning and fought a long, hard battle with Connlai. In the end, the older warrior won. As Connlai lay dying, he revealed his true identity to Cuchulainn, who was distraught but took the corpse of his son to show to the men of Ulster.

Another legend involving Cuchulainn predates the latter. It is the legend of the feast of BRICRIU. Bricriu, who was known for his love of mischief, organized a feast for the men of Ulster and Connacht, who were longtime rivals. At such feasts it was traditional for the most heroic warrior present to carve the roast meat. Bricriu, living up to his reputation for mischief, suggested to each of three warriors that he should claim the honour. The three were Cuchulainn,

Conall Cernach and Laoghaire Buadhach. An argument broke out as to which of these was the most worthy, and it was decided to refer the decision to MEDB, queen of Connacht. She chose Cuchulainn, but the other two refused to accept her decision, accusing him of bribing the queen. Having failed to resolve the problem in this way, all three candidates for the honour sought the help of CU ROI MAC DAIRI, king of Munster. He, too, chose Cuchulainn and, once again, the other two contenders refused to accept the decision. Next, a giant entered the contest. He challenged all three to cut off his head and then the following evening to allow him to return and cut off the head of the relevant contestant. Laoghaire Buadhach and Conall Cernach cut off the head of the giant and clearly assumed that he would then be dead. When he duly reappeared, Laoghaire and Conall both reneged on their agreements, but when it came to Cuchulainn, he duly beheaded the giant and then knelt down and offered his neck to the giant to be beheaded himself. The giant then revealed himself as Cu Roi mac Dairi and indicated that what had happened had simply confirmed him in his original judgement that Cuchulainn was the greatest warrior of the three and so should carve the roast.

Cu Roi mac Dairi appears in other legends with Cuchulainn. In one, Cuchulainn led his men on a raid to what is variously indicated as the OTHERWORLD or Scotland. The Munster king, who was noted for his SHAPE-CHANGING powers, appeared in disguise and offered to help them on condition that any of the spoils from the raid were shared with him.

CUCHULAINN

When the raiding party succeeded in acquiring a magic CAULDRON, three magic cows and a beautiful Otherworld maiden known as Blathnad, Cuchulainn and his men went back on their promise and refused to share the spoils with the unidentified stranger. Cu Roi mac Dairi then revealed himself and seized all the spoils. When Cuchulainn attempted to prevent him doing this, the Munster king buried Cuchulainn up to his armpits and shaved off all his hair. Obviously humiliated, Cuchulainn vowed revenge. He entered into a conspiracy with Blathnad, whom Cu Roi mac Dairi had married, and succeeded in killing him. Blathnad was killed when the FILI of Cu Roi mac Dairi pulled her over a cliff with him so that they both met their deaths on the rocks below.

Cuchulainn played a major part in the hostilities between Ulster and Connacht, when MEDB of Connacht was intent on acquiring DONN CUAILGNE, the great brown bull of Ulster. When Medb and her forces invaded Ulster, most of the Ulstermen were suffering from a kind of illness that made them too weak to fight, the illness being the result of a curse put on them by MACHA. Cuchulainn was unaffected by the curse and so was strong enough to fight heroically and single-handedly against the Connacht army.

Various legends surround the death of Cuchulainn. He had chosen fame instead of long life and so was destined to die young. Medb is said to have used the magic of the posthumous children of CALATIN to help weaken him when he went into battle with Erc, the battle that led to his death. According to some sources, Cuchulainn, realizing that he was dying, tied himself to a pillar so that he would die erect and honourably, BADB, in the form of a RAVEN, perching on his shoulder to indicate his imminent death.

He is said to have broken bonds and ignored supernatural warnings before going into his last battle. He was forced, perhaps by the magic powers of his enemies, to eat dog flesh and so was physically weakened. He ignored the fact that his horse cried tears of blood as he prepared for battle, although this was a warning of doom. He saw someone washing his armour in the river and failed to realize that this was presaging his doom.

Although married to Emer, Cuchulainn was also involved with several other women. One of these was FAND. He is said to have rejected sexual advances made to him by MORRIGAN and to have incurred her hostility thereafter. *See also* HEAD.

CULHWCH

In Welsh Celtic mythology, Culhwch was the son of Cilydd and Goleuddydd. For the story of his birth, *see* GOLEUDDYDD. When his mother died, his father married again, although his mother had begged him not to and had tried to arrange that he would not. His stepmother wanted Culhwch to marry her daughter and, when he refused, she was furious and put a curse on him that the only woman that he could marry was OLWEN. The problem was that Olwen was the daughter of the giant YSPADDADEN. Culhwch had first of all to find Olwen, and he gathered together a group of people, each chosen for a particular skill, to help him. After various adventures, they met the aunt of Culhwch, his dead mother's sister, who agreed to arrange a meeting between Olwen and Culhwch. When they met, Olwen agreed to marry him but pointed out that he would have to ask her father for her hand in marriage and he would be likely to impose stringent conditions.

She was right, but first Culhwch had to meet Yspaddaden. On three successive days he and his companions went to the giant's castle to try to gain entrance and speak to him. On each of the days the giant told them that they would have to come back the following day and, as they turned to go, threw a great poisoned spear or stone after them. Culhwch and his companions always succeeded in catching the missile and in throwing it back. According to one legend, the poisoned object hit Yspaddaden in the chest and then in the eye. On the fourth day, the giant agreed to the marriage between the two young people but set Culhwch a series of extremely difficult tasks. The number of the tasks varies from source to source, but they were all incredibly difficult, being able to be performed only with supernatural help, and the giant kept imposing other conditions. According to one legend, Culhwch, having completed the tasks but still meeting with opposition, finally grew extremely angry with Yspaddaden and gathered an army together to storm his castle. The giant was killed and Culhwch at last was able to marry Olwen.

CULLAN *see* Cuchulainn.

CUMHAILL *see* Fionn mac Cumhaill; Goll mac Morna; Uigreann.

CU ROI MAC DAIRI
In Irish Celtic mythology, Cu Roi mac Dairi was a king of Munster and a sorcerer. He was involved in several legends relating to CUCHULAINN.

CYMIDEI CYMEINFOLL *see* LLASSAR LLAESGYNEWID.

D

DA DERGA'S HOSTEL

In Irish Celtic mythology, Da Derga's Hostel was owned by a Leinster chief. A hostel was a place where travellers were always welcome, and Da Derga's Hostel was the place to which CONAIRE MOR insisted on travelling, having broken a GEIS or bond by so doing. He is also said to have ignored warnings of doom on his way there. He is said to have met three riders dressed in red and mounted on red horses, which were harbingers of death. Despite the fact that his journey to Da Derga's Hostel was foredoomed, he persisted. On his arrival at the hostel, his enemies attacked him and his men and, although they succeeded in destroying many of the enemy, Conaire was killed and the hostel destroyed

DAGHDA *or* DAGDA, THE

In Irish Celtic mythology, the Daghda, whose name meant 'the good god' and which has various variants, was a father-god and the chief of the TUATHA DE DANANN. He was the son of Eladu.

He is often depicted as a very large man wearing peasant garb, in particular a short tunic that reveals his buttocks. The Celts may have chosen to present him in this way to emphasize his sexuality and fertility, since his sexuality is demonstrated in some of the legends concerning him. For example, he is said to have mated with MORRIGAN before the second Battle of MAGH TUIREDH as she stood with one foot on each bank of the River Unius and also with BOANN in an illicit union that produced OENGHUS.

According to legend, the Daghda always carried a gigantic club that had magical powers. One end of the club was destructive and was used to kill his enemies, but the other end had magical healing powers and could heal the wounded and even revive the dead. It was so huge that, although the Daghda could wield it without any difficulty, it had to be dragged around on wheels for ease of transport. As well as being associated with this magic club, the Daghda is associated with a magic CAULDRON. This had an inexhaustible supply of food and no one went away from it feeling hungry. Like the club, it had healing powers and could heal the wounded and restore the dead to life. The Daghda is also said to have been the owner of a magic HARP that was stolen by the FOMORII but was recovered.

As his possession of an inexhaustible cauldron suggests, the Daghda was associated with abundance. Although he was a very powerful figure, being the chief of the Tuatha, he was not presented as a very attractive but as fat and gross. He is supposed to have had a prodigious appetite for food as well as sex, and this is demonstrated by a legend relating to an attempt by the Fomorii to increase their chances of success at the second Battle of MAGH TUIREDH. They somehow persuaded the Daghda to eat from a cauldron of porridge just before the battle. It was no ordinary cauldron but one with no bottom, and so its contents went deep into the ground. Legend has it that the amount of porridge it held was equivalent to eighty cauldrons and that it contained whole pigs, sheep and goats. The Daghda ate it all with a spoon large enough to hold a man and a woman, and showed absolutely no signs of having overeaten.

The Tuatha De Danann defeated the Fomorii, but they themselves were conquered by the Sons of MIL ESPAINE. After their defeat, the Tuatha were assigned the underground part of Ireland while the Sons of Mil Espaine ruled the upper part of the country. The Daghda gave each of the Tuatha a SIDH underground and is then said to have resigned as chief, handing over the leadership to BODB DEARG, who was a son of the Daghda

DAIRE

In Irish Celtic mythology, Daire was a son of FIONN MAC CUM-HAILL. Legend has it that he was swallowed by a monster but succeeded in hacking his way out of the creature's stomach, thereby releasing other people who had also been swallowed.

DANA *see* DANU.

DANU *or* DANA

In Irish Celtic mythology, Danu was a MOTHER-GODDESS and the mother of the TUATHA DE DANANN.

DANI

Dani was one of the last Celtic kings to rule at TARA before the arrival of St PATRICK. He led a military campaign into Britain and then into Europe. He was struck by lightning when he was storming a tower in the Rhine valley.

DEALGNAID

In Irish Celtic mythology, Dealgnaid was the wife of PARTHOLAN. She is said to have accompanied him to Ireland. She was the mother of RURY, who is said by some to have been the son of her husband, Partholan, but may have been the son of TOPA, the manservant of Partholan whom Dealgnaid seduced.

DECAPITATION *see* HEAD, THE.

DEICHTIRE *or* DEICHTINE

In Irish Celtic mythology, Deichtire is said to have been the daughter of the druid CATHBAD and the mother of CUCHULAINN, perhaps by the god LUGH, although she was married to SUALTAM, an Ulster chieftain, and some sources say that Cuchulainn was his son. Some sources indicate that she was the daughter or sister of CONCHOBAR MAC NESSA.

DEIRDRE *or* DERDRIU

In Irish Celtic mythology, Deirdre was the subject of a prophesy by the druid CATHBAD. He forecast that she would become the fairest woman in all of Ireland but that she would bring death and destruction to the country. Because of the second part of this prophecy, some people wanted to have her killed at birth. However, CONCHOBAR MAC NESSA, hearing of the prophecy of her beauty, decreed that she should live and that he would marry her when she came of age. When she did come of age, she did not want to marry Conchobar, who was by that time quite old, and wanted to marry NAOISE instead.

Legend has it that Deirdre saw a RAVEN drinking the blood of a newly killed calf on snowy ground and remarked that she could love a man whose hair was as black as the feathers of the raven, whose skin was as white as the snow, and whose blood was as red as that of the calf. She was told that Naoise answered to this description, and she contrived to meet him one day as he rode through the woods. She fell in love with him and wanted to marry him. He, however, was reluctant to get involved with her because of her betrothal to Conchobar and also because of the prophesy that she would bring death and destruction to Ireland, although he could not but be impressed by her beauty. Deirdre was determined to have him. She is said to have threatened that she would make him a laughing stock if he did not become her lover, and he agreed to elope with her to Alba, or Scotland, in the company of his two brothers. There they lived in exile for several years until Conchobar had been supposedly persuaded to forgive them and offer them an amnesty if they returned to Ireland. FERGUS MAC ROTH was sent as part of a group to ask them to return home and promise them safety when they did. Naoise trusted Fergus, but Deirdre foresaw doom. When they reached Ireland, Conchobar broke his word and had Naoise and his brothers killed by Eoghan mac Durthacht. Fergus was furious at Conchobar's treachery, and with a group of men attacked EMHAIN MACHA, killed many Ulstermen and defected to MEDB of Connacht, Conchobar's enemy.

Conchobar married Deirdre against her will, and, after a year that she spent pining and never smiling, he was so angry with her that he gave her to Eoghan mac Durthacht. As she was travelling by chariot to the house of Eoghan, her hands tied to prevent her escaping, she threw herself from the chariot and dashed her head against a rock. The blow killed her. After she was buried, a pine tree began to grow from her grave and a similar pine tree began to grow from Naoise's grave so that the two trees intertwined.

DEMNA *see* Fionn mac Cumhaill.

DEOCA
In Irish Celtic mythology, Deoca was engaged to be married to Lairgnen. She begged him to bring her the singing swans who were actually the children of Lir, whose stepmother had turned into swans because she was jealous of them. Just as he trapped the swans and brought them to Deoca, the period of transformation of nine hundred years ended and the swans began to revert to their human form. They were no longer young but old and wizened, and Lairgnen fled in terror.

DERDRIU *see* Deirdre.

DEVORGILLA *or* DERBHORGILL
In Irish Celtic mythology, Devorgilla was about to be given as tribute to the Fomorii when she was rescued by Cuchulainn. Devorgilla and her handmaidens changed themselves into swans so that they could follow Cuchulainn, Devorgilla having fallen in love with him. Not realizing this, Cuchulainn or his companion brought down one of the swans with a slingshot.

At that, the swans resumed their human shape and Cuchulainn sucked the shot out of Devorgilla's wound. It duly healed but, because Cuchulainn had swallowed Devorgilla's blood, they were now united by blood ties and so could not marry.

DER GREINE *see* LAOGHAIRE MAC CRIMTHANN.

DIAN CECHT

In Irish Celtic mythology, Dian Cecht was the god of healing, often depicted as a giant leech. He was especially active during the two Battles of MAGH TUIREDH. After the first, he replaced the severed hand of NUADA with a silver one, and during the second he was kept busy plunging the dead and injured of the TUATHA DE DANANN into a magic CAULDRON or WELL to revive or heal them so that they were ready to fight again. His three sons were also healers, and one of them, Midach, showed such a gift for healing that Dian Cecht was afraid of having his own reputation surpassed and therefore killed him. He also killed MEICHE.

DIARMAID

In Irish Celtic mythology, there are several people called Diarmaid, but the most famous of these is Diarmaid ua Duibhne, who was the son of DONN and is said to have been either the foster son or grandson of OENGHUS. He received a spot, known as the 'love spot', on his forehead from a mysterious maiden who said that any woman who saw this spot would instantly fall in love with him. He is said to have been extremely handsome, and GRAINNE fell in love with him, although she was engaged to be married to the elderly FIONN

MAC CUMHAILL. At the wedding feast before her marriage, she drugged Fionn and most of those present and placed Diarmaid under a GEIS or bond to elope with her, some of those present acting as witnesses. Fionn and his followers followed them and besieged them in a wood. Oenghus rescued Grainne, and Diarmaid escaped by leaping over the heads of his attackers.

Although Diarmaid had eloped with Grainne, he still felt loyal to Fionn and for some time refused to have sexual relations with her. Eventually, because of her taunting of him, he agreed, and the couple had four children.

With the help of Oenghus, Fionn became supposedly reconciled with Diarmaid and Grainne. Diarmaid went hunting with Fionn to kill the magic boar, BEANN GHULBAN, although it had been prophesied that this boar, the foster-brother of Diarmaid, would kill him. Diarmaid killed the boar but was himself mortally wounded. Fionn could have saved him with water from his own hands, since he had the gift of healing, but twice, remembering how Diarmaid and Grainne had betrayed him, he let the water trickle through his fingers and by the time that he had fetched a third amount of water Diarmaid had died.

DON

In Welsh Celtic mythology, Don was the Welsh equivalent of the Irish DANU. She is said to have been the daughter of MATHONWY, and so the sister of MATH, and the wife of BELI. Her children include GWYDION, GILFAETHWY and ARANRHOD.

DONN

There are various people called Donn in Irish Celtic mythology. Of these, one is the god of death. Another was one of the Sons of MIL ESPAINE, and he is sometimes identified with the god of death. In terms of the invasion of Ireland by the Sons of Mil Espaine, he is better known as EBER DONN.

Donn was also the name of the father of DIARMAID ua Duibhne. His wife had an affair with ROC, and Donn crushed the child to death in a fit of rage. The child was brought back to life but in the form of the monstrous boar that killed Diarmaid, BEANN GHULBAN.

DONN CUAILGNE
In Irish Celtic mythology, Donn Cuailgne was the name of the great brown BULL of Ulster. It was at the centre of the TAIN BO CUAILGNE, the legend of how MEDB tried to get hold of it and caused a war between Ulster and Connacht. The bull was finally captured and was taken to Medb's camp, where it had a terrible fight with FINNBHENACH, the white-horned bull of Connacht, during which Finnbhenach was killed and torn to pieces. After that, Donn Cuailgne went back to Ulster, where it died.

DRUID
In Celtic culture, a druid was a priest. The name druid is thought to have come from *drus*, the ancient name for the oak tree, which was sacred to the druids. As well as being priests, the druids were teachers, poets, philosophers, seers and judges. Druids represented the most powerful force in Celtic society. Druids were extremely highly trained and this rigorous training could go on for as long as twenty years.

DUBH LACHA *see* MONGAN.

DUN-TRI-LAG *see* SAMHAIR.

DURROW *see* ILLUMINATED GOSPELS.

DYFED
In Welsh Celtic mythology, the realm over which PWYLL reigned.

DYLAN EIL TON
In Welsh Celtic mythology, Dylan Eil Ton was a golden-haired boy who was the first of the two sons to be born to ARANRHOD when she was taking the virginity test for the post of footholder to MATH. At the moment of his birth he made for the sea where he was able to swim like a fish. 'Eil ton' indicates 'son of the wave'.

E

EACHTACH
In Irish Celtic mythology, Eachtach was the daughter of GRAINNE and DIARMAID ua Duibhne. She attacked FIONN MAC CUMHAILL, who had wanted to marry her mother and who had pursued her parents for many years, so severely that it took him four years to recover from his wounds.

EACHTRA *see* ECHTRAI.

EANNA
In Irish Celtic mythology, Eanna was the father of SGATHACH. When he was visiting Eanna's SIDH, FIONN MAC CUMHAILL said that he would marry Sgathach for a year, but the girl played a tune on her magic harp when Fionn and his men lay asleep and next day they woke to find themselves far from Eanna's sidh with no way of returning.

EASAL *see* PIGS.

EBER *or* EBER DONN
In Irish Celtic mythology, Eber was one of the leaders of the expedition undertaken by the Sons of MIL ESPAINE to Ireland. He killed MAC CUILL, but he himself was dead before his

brother, EBER FINN, and Eremon quarrelled over who should rule Ireland.

EBER FINN
In Irish Celtic mythology, Eber Finn was one of the leaders of the expedition made by the sons of MIL ESPAINE to Ireland. He was the brother of EBER DONN, who killed MAC CUILL. After the death of his brother, Eber Finn became involved in a dispute with EREMON, another of the leaders of the Sons of Mil Espaine, over who should be ruler of Ireland. AMHAIRGHIN decreed that Eremon should rule first and that Eber Finn should become ruler on the death of Eremon. Eber Finn refused to accept this judgement, and Ireland was divided into two realms. The southern part was given to Eber Finn and the northern part to Eremon. This was not really acceptable to either of them, but they agreed to the division. However, before long war broke out and Eber Finn was killed. Eremon became king of all Ireland which he ruled from TARA.

ECHID
In Irish Celtic mythology, Echid was the grandfather of CONCHOBAR MAC NESSA.

ECHTRAI *or* EACHTRA
In Irish Celtic mythology, echtrai referred to a class of adventure legends usually relating to a mortal's journey to the OTHERWORLD, made either by crossing several tracts of WATER or by entering a SIDH. *See* IMMRAM.

EDAIN *see* ETAIN.

EDAIN ECHRAIDHE *see* HORSES.

EFRAWG *see* PEREDUR.

EFNISIEN

In Welsh Celtic mythology, Efnisien was the brother of NISIEN and the half-brother of BENDIGEID VRAN, also known as Bran the Blessed, BRANWEN and the rest of the children of LLYR. He was known as a mischief-maker, and his brother Nisien was known as a peacemaker. When MATHOLWCH went from Ireland to Wales to seek the hand of Branwen in marriage, Efnisien inflicted terrible disfigurement on the hundred horses that Matholwch had brought with him. Matholwch regarded this as a terrible insult to him and took his revenge by ill-treating Branwen when he got her to Ireland. Bendigeid Vran was angry at his sister's treatment and formed an expedition to go to Ireland to rescue her.

On his arrival in Ireland, the Irish at first pretended to be pleased to see him and put a splendid palace at his disposal. However, a hundred warriors had been hidden inside bags of provisions and were all set to jump out and attack the Welsh party when the time was ripe. The cunning Efnisien, however, suspected what had happened and crushed the heads of the warriors while they were still in the bags.

It was decided between Matholwch and Bendigeid that the best way of ending their dispute was to bestow the sovereignty of Ireland on GWERN, the son of Branwen and Matholwch. Efnisien caused more trouble by taking the boy and throwing him into a blazing fire. A terrible war broke out. At first the Welsh were being badly defeated because they had the magic CAULDRON that Bendigeid had given Matholwch as a wedding present and that could restore any wounded Irish warriors to health and any dead Irish warriors to life. Efnisien succeeded in destroying the cauldron but he was killed while doing so. Both sides suffered many terrible casualties in the war. Only seven of Bendigeid's expedition returned across the Irish Sea, and five pregnant women, who had remained hidden in a cave, were all that were left of the Irish.

EGGARDON *see* HILL FORT.

EIRE
The name given to southern Ireland today is Eire. The name derives from the goddess ERIU.

EISIRT
In Irish Celtic mythology, Eisirt was the bard at the court of IUBDAN, king of the FAYLINN, a diminutive people. It was Eisirt who placed Iubdan under a bond to visit Ulster where, he said, there was a race of giants who were more powerful than the Faylinns. Iubdan did not believe Eisirt, and so Eisirt went to Ulster to the court of FERGUS MAC LEDA and returned with AEDA. He was a dwarf at the court of Fergus and so extremely small by Ulster's standards but he was huge by the standards of the people of Faylinn. It was then that Eisirt put Iubdan under a bond to visit Ulster. When he did so he, with his wife BEBO, were taken captive and had great difficulty escaping.

EITHNE (1) *see* ELCMAR.

EITHNE (2) *see* ETHLINN.

ELADU
In Irish Celtic mythology, Eladu was the father of the DAGHDA.

ELATHA
In Irish Celtic mythology Elatha was a FOMORII leader who had an affair with Eri, one of the TUATHA DE DANANN women. She gave birth to BRES as a result of this affair. Bres later became king of the Tuatha De Danann.

ELCMAR
In Irish Celtic mythology, Elcmar was the foster-father of OENGHUS, a god of love. Legend has it that the DAGHDA sent Elcmar on a journey so that he could have a sexual relationship with Elcmar's wife, Eithne or Ethne, although obviously he came up with some other reason for the journey. Elcmar's wife bore the Daghda a son, although Elcmar did not know this. The boy was Oenghus. There is some confusion with this legend, as there is with several others. One legend has it that Elcmar's wife was BOANN but others say that she was his sister.

ELEN
In Welsh Celtic mythology, Elen was the daughter of Eudaf, from whom the kings of Cornwall are supposed to be descended. She is said to have been married to MACSEN WLEDIG and to have returned to Wales after his death to devote herself to Christian good works.

ELFFIN

In Welsh Celtic mythology, Elffin was the boy who found the leather bag containing TALIESIN in his father's fish weir, where CERRIDWEN had thrown it. He it was who named Taliesin because of his 'radiant brow'.

EMER

In Irish Celtic mythology, Emer was the daughter of FORGALL and the wife of CUCHULAINN. She did not have an easy time in her marriage as Cuchulainn was loved by many other women. Just before his death, Cuchulainn had a vision of his wife being thrown from the burning ramparts of EMHAIN MACHA. He hurried to her, but in fact she was perfectly all right. She tried to persuade him to stay with her, but he refused and set off on what proved to be the road to his death. His vision of Emer's danger had in fact been a warning of his own doom.

EMHAIN MACHA

The seat of the kings of ULSTER was known as Emhain Macha, which was the centre of the RED BRANCH. It is supposed to have been established by MACHA, hence its name. It was the court of CONCHOBAR MAC NESSA.

EOCHAIDH AIREMH

In Irish Celtic mythology, Eochaidh Airemh married the reincarnation of ETAIN and then refused to return her to MIDHIR, her husband, in her original form. For details of this rather complex legend, *see* MIDHIR.

EOGHAN MAC DURTHACHT *see* DEIRDRE; NAOISE.

EPONA

In Gaulish Celtic mythology, Epona was one of the more important deities. Epona derives from the Celtic word for 'horse' and she was a horse-goddess. Since HORSES were of particular importance to the Celts, in terms of transport, war and economics, it follows that the cult of a horse-goddess was an important part of their beliefs. Epona is always depicted with horses. In some representations she is shown riding side-saddle and in others she is standing or sitting between two or more horses. She is also often shown with a symbol of fertility or abundance, for example a basket of fruit or corn. Her horse is always a mare, and this is sometimes shown with a foal, representing fertility and regeneration. Epona also seems to have been associated with healing, particularly water healing, being venerated at some Gaulish SPRING sanctuaries. She is also thought to have been associated with death, and it has been suggested that perhaps she was a guide and guardian to those of her devotees who were entering the next world.

ERC

In Irish Celtic mythology, Erc features in a legend in which he is said to have killed CUCHULAINN. He joined forces with MEDB and the monstrous children of CALATIN and marched in battle against Cuchulainn.

EREMON

In Irish Celtic mythology, Eremon was one of the Sons of MIL ESPAINE who invaded Ireland. On the death of EBER (Donn) he had a quarrel with EBER FINN over who should rule Ireland.

The country was first divided between them but war broke out and Eber Finn was killed. Eremon thus became the first king to rule over all Ireland.

ERI *see* BRES; ELATHA.

ERIU
In Irish Celtic mythology, Eriu was the goddess who gave her name to Ireland. Legend has it that she was one of a triad of goddesses who met the Sons of MIL ESPAINE when they arrived in Ireland and asked if their names could be given to the country, promising the invaders that Ireland would be theirs forever if they agreed. AMHAIRGHIN promised that the country would be named Eire. Eriu is one of the three aspects of the sovereignty of Ireland, the other two being Fotla or Fodla and Banbha or Banb.

ESIAS
In Irish Celtic mythology, Esias was a wizard who lived in GORIAS. He is said to have presented the invincible spear to LUGH and to have been one of the wizards who taught magical arts to the TUATHA DE DANANN.

ESTRILDIS *see* HABREN.

ETAIN *or* **EDAIN**
In Irish Celtic mythology Etain was the daughter of AILILL. MIDHIR fell in love with her and sought her hand in marriage, using the auspices of OENGHUS to intercede on his behalf. However, Midhir reckoned without his first wife, FUAMNACH, who was extremely jealous of his new love and turned her into

various shapes in order to destroy the marriage. The legend is a complex one and details of it are given under the entry on MIDHIR.

ETHAL ANUBAL
In Irish Celtic mythology, Ethal Anubal was a prince of Connacht and the father of CAER. He was thus the father-in-law of OENGHUS. When Oenghus sought Caer's hand in marriage, Ethal told him that his best chance of success was to turn himself into a swan on one of the alternate years that Caer turned into a swan.

ETHLINN *or* EITHNE *or* ETHNE
In Irish Celtic mythology, Ethlinn was the daughter of BALOR. Because of a prophecy that he would be killed by his grandson, Balor had her confined in a tower, probably the GLASS TOWER. CIAN succeeded in entering the tower and having a relationship with Ethlinn. There are variations on the legend. According to one source, she bore one son, whom Balor ordered to be drowned, but the boy was saved and fostered by MANANNAN MAC LIR. The boy was LUGH, and he fulfilled the prophecy. According to another source, she gave birth to triplets and all but one was drowned, the surviving child being brought up by Cian.

ETHNE (1) *see* ELCMAR.

ETHNE (2) *see* ETHLINN.

ETHNE (3) *see* RONAN.

EUDAF *see* ELEN.

EUROSSWYD
In Welsh Celtic mythology, Eurosswyd was the father of EFNISIEN and NISIEN by PENARDUN.

F

FACHTNA
In Irish Celtic mythology, Fachtna was the king of ULSTER and the husband or lover of NESSA. According to some sources, he was the father of CONCHOBAR MAC NESSA, although other sources indicate that Conchobar was the son of the druid CATHBAD, who had an affair with Nessa.

FALIAS
In Irish Celtic mythology, Falias was one of the four great dities of the TUATHA DE DANANN before they went to Ireland. It was the home of MORFESSA.

FAND
In Irish Celtic mythology, Fand was a daughter of Aed Abrat and sister of LI BAN. She was the wife of MANANNAN MAC LIR. One legend has it that when he left her she was attacked by three FOMORII warriors. Her sister Li Ban went to CUCHULAINN to ask him to protect her sister on condition that Fand rewarded him by becoming his lover. Cuchulainn duly arrived and defended Fand from her enemies. He then became her lover before returning to his wife, EMER. Emer found out about his affair with Fand and made an attempt on her life when she tried to make another assignation with Cuchulainn. Accord-

ing to the legend, Fand's husband found out about all of this and arrived to demand that Fand choose between him and her lover. Fand chose her husband.

FANNELL *see* NECHTA SCENE.

FAYLINN
In Irish Celtic mythology, Faylinn was the kingdom of diminutive people who were ruled over by IUBDAN. *See also* EISIRT.

FEBAL *see* BRAN (1).

FERDIA
In Irish Celtic mythology, Ferdia was the foster brother and friend of CUCHULAINN. When MEDB invaded Ulster to get hold of DONN CUAILGNE, the great brown bull of Ulster, he took her side, although Cuchulainn was on the side of the Ulstermen, most of whom were under some kind of curse and were too ill to fight against Medb's Connacht men. Ferdia was unwilling to fight his friend, but legend has it that he was goaded into single combat with Cuchulainn. Ferdia was killed by Cuchulainn, who was grief-stricken.

FERGUS MAC LEDA
In Irish Celtic mythology, Fergus mac Leda was the king of Ulster at the time that IUBDAN and his wife went from FAYLINN to visit Ulster to see for themselves what was to them a race of GIANTS.

FERGUS MAC ROTH
In Irish Celtic mythology, Fergus mac Roth was a king of

Ulster. He was in love with NESSA, the widow of his brother, FACHTNA, but she would agree to have a sexual relationship with him only if he gave up his throne for a year to her son, CONCHOBAR MAC NESSA. This he agreed to, but at the end of the year Conchobar refused to give the throne up, and, in any case, he had proved to be a popular king. At first Fergus served Conchobar, but he was disgusted when Conchobar broke his word to NAOISE, having offered him an amnesty to return to Ireland from Scotland after he had eloped with Deirdre, and had him and his brothers killed. Fergus had been one of the ambassadors sent to offer a supposed pardon to Naoise. Fergus then defected to MEDB, the queen of Connacht, and took part in the TAIN BO CUAILGNE on the side of the men of Connacht. He was the tutor and foster father of CUCHULAINN, and fulfilled his promise to him never to confront his foster son in battle, thus having to leave Medb's army.

Fergus is said to have been fond of the good life, feasting in particular. He is also said to have been promiscuous and the lover of the promiscuous Medb. According to one legend, he was killed by AILILL when he was bathing in a pool with Medb.

FERREX

In British Celtic mythology, Ferrex was a son of GORBODUC and JUDON and the brother of PORREX. Porrex and Ferrex had a quarrel over the succession, and Porrex plotted to ambush Ferrex. He, however, found out about this and escaped to Gaul to raise an army. This attempt to save his life was in vain, as Porrex killed him on his arrival back in Britain. Judon went mad on hearing of the death of Ferrex and hacked Porrex to pieces. Thus, on the death of Gorboduc, there was no one left to continue the line of descent, a line supposed to have come down from BRUTUS.

FIACHADH *see* KNIGHTS.

FIACHNA LURGAN *see* MONGAN.

FIACHNA MAC RETACH
In Irish Celtic mythology, Fiachna sought the help of LAOGHAIRE MAC CRIMTHANN to retrieve his wife and daughter, who had been abducted by GOLL of Magh Mell. Goll was killed by Laoghaire and the latter married Fiachna's daughter.

FIACHTRA
In Irish Celtic mythology, Fiachtra was a daughter of AOBH and LIR. She was one of the four children of Lir who were turned into swans by their stepmother, AOIFE, because she was jealous of their father's love for them. They were forced to spend nine hundred years as swans and retained their human form during the time of St Patrick, dying shortly thereafter.

FIANNA
In Irish Celtic mythology, the Fianna were a group of warriors who formed a military elite who guarded the high king of Ireland. At one point they were led by FIONN MAC CUMHAILL.

FIDCHELL
In Celtic legends, a game of chess often features, especially as a method of settling disputes. Although it is usually trans-

lated in the legends as 'chess', the game being referred to in Irish legends is usually fidchell, a board game resembling chess, said to have been invented by LUGH. The Welsh equivalent of the game was gwyddbwyll.

FILI (*PLURAL* FILIDH)

A fili was a bard or poet, often one who was attached to a royal court. A fili was a very learned person as well as being a poet, knowing much about heroic tales and genealogies as well as poetic metres, and often having the gift of prophesy. They fulfilled the function of poets, seers and royal advisers, and were often highly trained, many being trained in a special school for several years before being allowed to practise their art.

FINDABAIR *or* FINDABAR *or* FINDBHAIR

In Irish Celtic mythology, Findabair was the daughter of MEDB and AILILL. She fell in love with FRAOCH. Ailill is said not to have been in favour of the wedding and to have attempted to kill Fraoch. He persuaded him to swim in a lake and to fetch a branch from a rowan tree that grew above the lake. He was then asked to repeat the process, at which point a horrible monster, which was the guardian of the tree, attacked him. Although Fraoch was very badly wounded, he managed to gather his strength and succeeded in beheading the monster with a sword that the faithful Findabair threw him. Thus the attempts of Medb and Ailill to kill Fraoch failed. According to legend, Fraoch agreed to help Medb and Ailill in their quest for DONN CUAILGNE, the great brown bull of Ulster. During the course of the battle that ensued, Medb offered FERDIA Findabair's hand in marriage if he took part in single combat against CUCHULAINN, although whether or not Fraoch was dead by that time is not known. Ferdia was killed by Cuchulainn.

FINEGAS

In Irish Celtic mythology, Finegas was a druid to whom FIONN MAC CUMHAILL was sent to learn poetry and knowledge. It was either Fionn or Finegas who caught the SALMON OF KNOWL-EDGE, which Finegas had been trying to catch for some time. Finegas told Fionn to cook it, and he accidentally touched the hot salmon as it cooked with his thumb. Instinctively he put his thumb in his mouth to cool and soothe it, and thus was filled with the gift of knowledge and wisdom from the salmon.

FINIAS

In Irish Celtic mythology, Finias was one of the four great cities of the TUATHA DE DANANN before they went to Ireland. It was the home of USCIAS.

FINNBHENACH

In Irish Celtic mythology, Finnbhenach was the white-horned bull of Connacht. It was born into the herd owned by MEDB, but it transferred itself into the ownership of Medb's husband, AILILL, because it thought that it was beneath its dignity to belong to a herd owned by a woman. Medb was jealous of her husband's ownership of such a fine bull and decided that she must have DONN CUAILGNE, the great brown bull of Ulster, in order to outrival her husband. She invaded Ulster and a war took place. When Medb acquired the Donn Cuailgne, she took it back to her camp where it had a terrible fight with Finnbhenach, the fight lasting for a day and a night. Finnbhenach not only lost the fight but was reduced to pieces. *See also* TAIN BO CUAILGNE.

FINN MAC COOL *see* FIONN MAC CUMHAILL.

FINTAN
In Irish Celtic mythology, Fintan was the husband of CESAIR, the granddaughter of Noah, who led the first invaders to Ireland before the Flood. Her party consisted of fifty women and three men, Bith, Ladra and Fintan. When Ladra died, Bith and Fintan divided the women between them and Cesair became the wife of Fintan. When the Flood came, Fintan was the only survivor and he became an expert at SHAPE-CHANGING. According to one legend, he changed himself into the SALMON OF KNOWLEDGE.

FIONN MAC CUMHAILL
In Irish Celtic mythology, Fionn mac Cumhaill, sometimes anglicized as Finn mac Cool, was one of the most celebrated heroes. He was the son of Cumhaill, who fell in love with Muirne, the daughter of a DRUID. Her father opposed marriage between the two, and they eloped. Her father, according to legend, is then said to have sent GOLL after them. Cumhaill was killed by Goll, but Muirne bore him a posthumous son. He was called Demna, but he was so fair that he was renamed Fionn, which translates as 'fair'. There are many legends relating to Fionn.

At an early age he is said to have been sent to FINEGAS to

study poetry and gain knowledge. Finegas had long tried to catch the SALMON OF KNOWLEDGE, and eventually either he or Fionn caught it—legends differ as to which. When cooking it, Fionn burnt his thumb and sucked it, thereby becoming imbued with the gift of knowledge from the fish, and it was said thereafter that he had only to suck his thumb to have universal knowledge. Also at a young age, he is said to have killed the monster Aillen, a creature that every year at the feast of SAMHAIN went to the royal residence at TARA, lulled the guards asleep with magical music and burnt the place down. Fionn is said to have been able to resist the magical power of the music by pressing his spear to his forehead. He then drove off the monster and beheaded it. There are variations, and one legend has it that it was AMHAIRGHIN who succeeded in slaying the monster. Fionn was made head of the FIANNA.

Fionn had several wives and mistresses. One of these was SADB, who was turned into a fawn by a druid and who bore Fionn a son called OISIN. When he was quite old Fionn fell in love with GRAINNE and wanted to marry her. Grainne, who was much, much younger, reluctantly agreed, but arranged things so that she ran off with her beloved DIARMAID ua Duibhne. The enraged Fionn pursued them for years.

Fionn is known for his two faithful hounds, BRAN and SGEOLAN, who were really his nephews. They were the children of ILLAN and TUIREANN, but Illan's druid mistress had turned Tuireann into a wolfhound when she was pregnant and her sons were born as hounds.

Accounts of Fionn's death vary. One legend indicates that

he was killed by Aichleach during a rebellion of the Fianna. Another has it that he died at the age of 230 and that his death led to the decline and the disbanding of the Fianna. Yet another suggests that he was reincarnated as MONGAN, a seventh-century Irish chieftain, and still another suggests that the hero is not dead at all but is lying asleep in a cave waiting to help Ireland in her hour of need.

FIR BHOLG *or* FIRBOLG

In Irish Celtic mythology, Fir Bholg was the name given to the leaders of the invasion of Ireland after the NEMEDIANS. The name translates as 'bag men', and, according to one legend, they got their name because at one point they were slaves, perhaps in Thrace, and during their enslavement had to carry bags of soil from the fertile part of the country to the rocky, barren part. Another source suggests they took their name from a god, 'Bhuil'.

Some sources indicate that they were descendants of the Nemedians, who had gone to Thrace when they fled from Ireland, and some say that they are descended from SEMION. There were three groups of them, but they went under the general name of Fir Bholg. They are said to have divided Ireland into five provinces. The TUATHA DE DANANN ended the Fir Bholg's rule of Ireland when they defeated them at the first Battle of MAGH TUIREDH.

The vanquished Fir Bholg are said to have fled to Aran, but another source indicates that the Tuatha let them keep the Irish province of Connacht.

FIR DHOMHNANN *see* LEABHAR GABHALA EIREANN.

FIRE

The veneration of fire was important to the Celts. Bonfires were lit both at the festival of BELTANE on 1 May and at the festival of SAMHAIN on 1 November. The Celts may have thought of fire as the earthly element that corresponds to the SUN in the sky. WHEEL-rolling also played a part in the Celtic fire rituals, the wheels being set ablaze and rolled downhill. Another reported Celtic fire ritual suggests that the Celts went in for human SACRIFICE. Images in the human shape and made of wicker were supposedly filled with sacrificial animals and people and set alight.

FODLA *see* ERIU; MAC CECHT.

FOILL *see* NECHTA SCENE.

FOLLACH *see* TIGERNMAS.

FOMORII *or* **FOMHOIRE** *or* **FOMOIRE** *or* **FOMORIANS**
In Irish Celtic mythology, the Fomorii, a name that appears in various variant spellings, were a race of demonic beings, many of whom were half-human, half-monster, and many of whom had only one leg, one hand and a single eye in the middle of the forehead. Their name has been translated both as 'sea giants' and as 'under-demons', and they are thought to have had their home under the sea. They fought against PARTHOLAN when his forces invaded Ireland and were defeated by him, supposedly going into exile in the Hebrides and the Isle of Man. However, legend has it that they returned after NEMEDH's arrival in Ireland. They subjugated the Nemedians and ex-

torted terrible tributes from them, two-thirds of their corn, wine (some sources say milk), and children. The Nemedians rebelled but were defeated, and the few survivors fled, possibly to Greece or Thrace—the FIR BHOLG may be descendants of these survivors.

The next of the conflicts involving the Fomorii was against the TUATHA DE DANANN. At first both the Fomorii and the Tuatha De Danann inhabited Ireland, the Fomorii having quite a small part of it. The king of the Tuatha was NUADA, but he is said to have lost an arm at the first Battle of MAGH TUIREDH and was required to abdicate, there being a ruling that the leader of the Tuatha had to be physically perfect. His successor was BRES, who was in fact part Tuatha on his mother's side and part Fomorii on his father's side. Bres was a tyrannical ruler and was deposed, Nuada being reinstated after having had a silver arm fitted to replace his severed one. Bres was angry at being opposed and sought the help of the Fomorii. Hostilities broke out between the Fomorii and the Tuatha De Danann, and the second Battle of Magh Tuiredh took place. Both sides suffered heavy losses, but the Tuatha won, LUGH killing BALOR, the king of the Fomorii, by driving out his single eye with his slingshot. The Fomorii army was decimated and the remnants of the Fomorii people driven from Ireland.

FOOT-HOLDER *see* MATH FAB MATHONWY.

FORBAY

In Irish Celtic mythology, Forbay was the son of CONCHOBAR

MAC NESSA. He is said to have killed MEDB with a slingshot as she bathed in a lake on the island where she lived after the death of her husband, AILILL.

FORGALL

In Irish Celtic mythology, Forgall was the father of EMER, who married CUCHULAINN. Forgall was not keen on the union and made it a condition of the marriage that Cuchulainn went out of the country to study war skills at the house of SCATHACH. Secretly he hoped that Cuchulainn would not return but, of course, he did—and married Emer.

FOSTERING

In Celtic culture, fostering was common. Children would be fostered in the home of a druid, chief, scholar or monk from about the age of seven in order to be educated. They would learn about poetry, music and literature and often the skills necessary for warfare.

FOTLA *see* ERIU; MAC CECHT.

FRAOCH

In Irish Celtic mythology, Fraoch was a very handsome man who fell in love with FINDABAIR, the daughter of MEDB and AILILL. She returned his love, but her parents were reluctant for her to marry him and tried to kill him. Later he took part with Medb and Ailill in the quest for the DONN CUAILGNE.

FUAMNACH

In Irish Celtic mythology, Fuamnach was the first wife of MIDHIR. She was so jealous when Midhir fell in love with

ETAIN and took her for his wife that she turned the beautiful young woman into a series of shapes, starting with a pool of water.

FURBAIDHE *see* MEDB.

G

GABALINE
In Irish Celtic mythology, Gabaline was an ancient blind seer whom MEDB consulted when she wished to have details of the illness that had rendered the men of Ulster unfit for battle when she intended invading Ulster to bring back DONN CUAILGNE, the great brown bull of Ulster, to her home in Connacht.

GABHRA *or* **GOWRA**
In Irish Celtic mythology, the Battle of Gabhra, known also as Gowra, was the last great battle in which the FIANNA took part. It led to the loss of their supremacy in Ireland and to the death of most of them. The battle was instigated by CAIRBRE, who was intent on curbing the power of the Fianna. OSCAR, who was in command of the Fianna, killed Cairbre but was himself killed.

GAE-BHOLG
In Irish Celtic mythology, Gae-Bholg was the famous spear belonging to CUCHULAINN. Various stories attach to the spear. It was said to have been given to Cuchulainn by SCATHACH, who had taught him the skills of war. Known as 'the belly spear', it supposedly made one wound when it entered the body of an enemy but then it opened up into thirty barbs in-

side the body once it had gained entrance. Legend has it that the spear was supposed to be launched from between the toes. Cuchulainn used his spear to kill his foster brother FERDIA and his own son, CONNLAI, although he was unaware that he had been fighting his own son until after he had killed him.

GAELS
In Irish Celtic mythology, the Gaels were said to have been the descendants of the Sons of MIL ESPAINE, who defeated the TUATHA DE DANANN to become rulers of Ireland and the first human inhabitants of Ireland. In modern times the name is given to the inhabitants of Ireland and to the inhabitants of parts of Scotland, specifically those who speak Gaelic.

GAIBLE
In Irish Celtic mythology, Gaible was the son of NUADA. He stole a bundle of twigs that Ainge, a daughter of the DAGHDA, had gathered with which to build a tub for herself. Gaible threw the bundle of twigs away, having no use for them, and a mature wood sprang up where the twigs fell.

GAI DEARG
In Irish Celtic mythology, the name Gai Dearg was given to the magical red-handled spear owned by DIARMAID. He refused to take it on the hunt for BEANN GHULBAN because he felt it gave him an unfair advantage. GRAINNE had advised him to take it, and she proved to have been right to do so, as he was killed without it.

GALAHAD
In Welsh Celtic mythology, Galahad was originally known

as Gwalchafed, which translates as the 'falcon of summer'. In the medieval Arthurian legend, Galahad went in quest of the Holy GRAIL.

GALAN MAI
In Welsh Celtic culture, Galan Mai was the equivalent of the Irish BELTANE. Galan Mai was held on 1 May.

GALIAN
The ancient name for LEINSTER was Galian. *See* LAIGHIN.

GAILIOIN *or* GALIOIN
In Irish Celtic mythology, the Gailioin was one of the three companies that made up the descendants of NEMEDH, who came from Greece and invaded Ireland. *See also* LAIGHIN.

GAUL
Usually Gaul is thought of as corresponding to France, but the Gaul of the ancient Celts also included Switzerland and Belgium. As the Romans gradually conquered Gaul, some of the Celts were assimilated into Roman culture, some migrated, and many were killed.

GEIS
In Celtic mythology and culture, a geis was a kind of bond that people were placed under. If someone placed under such a bond broke it, he or she would either die or face extreme dishonour. The geis usually took the form of a prohibition of some kind.

GEOFFREY OF MONMOUTH
The base text for many of the stories in the medieval Arthurian saga is *Historia Regum Britanniae*, 'history of the kings of

Britain'. It was written by Geoffrey of Monmouth (*c*.1100–*c*.1155), a Welsh cleric of Breton origin.

GIANTS

In the legends of Celtic mythology, giants occur quite frequently. Traditionally giants could not be overcome by physical force because of their sheer size but had to be overcome by trickery or magic. Britain was supposed to have been ruled by a race of giants until the arrival of BRUTUS.

In the legends of the Celts, the word 'giant' appears not only to have been used in the sense of a huge person, many times the size of a normal person and often very ugly, but also in the sense of a person who has extraordinary talents and is thus superior to the ordinary person.

GIANTS' RING *see* MYRDDIN; STONEHENGE.

GILDAS

There is little in the way of written historical accounts relating to the Celts. One of the few extant records is *De Excidio Et Conquestu Britanniae*, 'On the Ruin and Conquest of Britain'. This is often attributed to Gildas, who is thought to have moved from what is now Strathclyde to go and live in Wales where he became a monk. The work with which he has been credited, although his authorship has been disputed, was probably written between 516 and 547 AD. The work is part history and part mythology, but it describes the invasion of Britain and the annihilation or mass migration of the Celts. He is also credited with the authorship of an open letter of rebuke to the secular and ecclesiastical Celts, *Epistola Gildae*.

GILFAETHWY

In Welsh Celtic mythology, Gilfaethwy was the son of DON. He fell in love with GOEWIN, who was then foot-holder at the court of MATH FAB MATHONWY and so a virgin, since only virgins could have the job of foot-holder. He confided his love to his brother, GWYDION, who set about helping his brother in his quest for Goewin. He decided that the first thing to do was to get Math away from his court, and with this in mind he brought about a quarrel between Math and PRYDERI so that the two would fight a war and Math would thus be absent from his court—only in times of war did Math not require the services of his foot-holder.

Gwydion asked Math for leave to go to Pryderi and ask him to present as a gift to Math a herd of magical swine that had been given to him by ARAWN. Math agreed, and Gwydion and Gilfaethwy went with some followers to the home of Pryderi, dressed as bards. After feasting with Pryderi, Gwydion offered to tell a story, and Pryderi was so delighted with it that he offered the supposed bard anything he liked in payment. The bard, alias Gwydion, chose the swine, but Pryderi explained that he had promised Arawn that he would not part with the swine until the herd had produced double its number. Gwydion then conjured up twelve magnificent horses and twelve magnificent hounds and offered to do an exchange. Pryderi agreed, but the next day the horses and hounds, which were magical illusions conjured up by Gwydion, disappeared, and Pryderi realized that he had been tricked. He thought that Math had been at the bottom of the trickery and set out to recover his swine from

him. Math saw Pryderi and his men approaching and
thought that they were going to invade his land. Thus Math
went to war and did not need the services of his foot-holder,
Goewin. The war was settled after two battles by the outcome of single combat between Pryderi and Gwydion, and
Gwydion used his magic powers to kill Pryderi.

Having thus cunningly got Math out of the way, Gwydion
accompanied his brother to Math's court to find Goewin.
One version of the legend has it that Gilfaethwy and
Gwydion then abducted Goewin and took it in turns to rape
her, and another has it that she was forced against her will to
marry Gilfaethwy. Either way, they had behaved deceitfully
and Gilfaethwy had had intercourse with a virginal foot-
holder. Math was furious and condemned them to change
shape each year. One year they were deer, the next year they
were swine and the next year they were wolves. Each year,
although they were both men as humans, they had to produce an offspring in the shape that they were. At the end of
three years, he considered that they had been punished
enough and changed them back into human shape.

GIONA MAC LUGHA

In Irish Celtic mythology, Giona mac Lugha was the son of
the warrior daughter of FIONN MAC CUMHAILL, who became a
leader of the FIANNA. He was far from being a good leader,
being lazy, inefficient and vain, and his men refused to fight
under him. Fionn took him in hand and taught him the qualities of leadership so that he became one of the Fianna's great
champions.

GIRALDUS CAMBRENSIS *see* ITINIERARIUM CAMBRIAE.

GLAS GHAIBHNENN
In Irish Celtic mythology, Glas Ghaibhnenn was a magic cow that was stolen by BALOR. He took it to TORY ISLAND, but CIAN went in pursuit and rescued the cow.

GLASS TOWER *or* **GLASS CASTLE**
In Irish Celtic mythology, the FOMORII are said to have built a glass tower or castle, also known as Conan's Tower, on TORY ISLAND. The NEMEDIANS stormed the island and castle, and killed CONAN MAC FEBAR, the king of the Fomorii. BALOR is said to have imprisoned his daughter in the Glass Tower.

GLASTONBURY *see* JOSEPH OF ARIMATHEA.

GLASTONBURY TOR
In Irish Celtic mythology, the hill at Glastonbury in the Vale of Avalon in Somerset, known as Glastonbury Tor, was said to be the home of GWYN AP NUDD and to have been a kind of gate between the mortal world and the OTHERWORLD. Celtic hermits occupied cells on the slopes of the hill. The Celtic name for Glastonbury Tor was Ynys Wittrin, meaning 'island of glass'. *See also* HILL SITES.

GLIFIEU
In Irish Celtic mythology, Glifieu was one of the seven survivors of the expedition that was mounted by BENDIGEID VRAN, or Bran the Blessed, to go to Ireland and retrieve BRANWEN, who was being ill-treated by her husband, MATHOLWCH. The other survivors included PRYDERI.

GOAT

In Celtic mythology and beliefs, the goat was a representation of fertility. A goat is sometimes depicted as accompanying the Romano-Celtic god Mercury, and the goat seems in some aspects to have been interchangeable with the RAM, also a representation of fertility. Like the ram, the goat also had associations with aggression, particularly sexual aggression. Horned gods were a common part of Celtic culture. Often these HORNS were representations of RAM's horns and often they were representations of deer antlers but sometimes they were goat's horns.

GOEWIN

In Welsh Celtic mythology, Goewin was the beautiful daughter of Pebin. She was given the post of foot-holder to MATH FAB MATHONWY, a post that could only be held by a virgin. Her beauty excited the admiration and love of GILFAETHWY. His brother, GWYDION, used his wiles and magic skills to get Math out of the way. According to one version of the legend, Gilfaethwy then forced Goewin to marry him, and according to another Gilfaethwy and Gwydion raped Goewin. Math was furious and condemned Gilfaethwy and Gwydion to three years of SHAPE-CHANGING.

GOFANNON

In Welsh Celtic mythology, Gofannon is a divine SMITH and the Welsh equivalent of the Irish GOIBHNIU. He is said to have struck the blow that killed his nephew DYLAN EIL TON, the son of ARANRHOD, although other reasons are also given for his death.

GOIBHNIU

In Irish Celtic mythology, Goibhniu was a SMITH god. He was a member of a triad of craft gods who were associated with the TUATHA DE DANANN, the other two being Creidhne and LUCHTA, Creidhne being the metalworker and Luchta being the wright or carpenter. The three craft gods were responsible for making and repairing the magic weapons of the Tuatha De Danann, which inflicted wounds from which no one could recover. Goibhniu is said to have been the host at feasts in the OTHERWORLD at which people who partook of a special ale became immortal.

GOLEUDDYDD

In Welsh Celtic mythology, Goleuddydd was the wife of Cilydd and mother of CULHWCH. While she was pregnant with him, she became mad and wandered aimlessly around the countryside. She is said to have become rational again when she went into labour, but, discovering that she was in field in the middle of a herd of swine, she became extremely afraid, and fear made her give birth immediately. Her son was named after his birthplace because in Welsh *hwch* means 'pigs'. According to one version of the legend, Goleuddydd was so scared that she abandoned the baby amid the pigs and ran off, Culhwch being found by the swineherd and taken to the home of the baby's father.

Another part of the legend concerning Goleuddydd indicates that she knew that she was going to die and was afraid that her husband would remarry and that her son would be dispossessed if he had other children by his second wife.

She made Cilydd promise that he would not remarry until a briar with two heads grew from her grave. In order to prevent such a thing happening, she instructed a monk who was her personal confessor to check for any sign of such a plant appearing on her grave and to pull it out if such appeared. After seven years, the monk became negligent and a briar with two heads grew on Goleuddydd's grave. Cilydd duly married again. For the rest of the story, *see* CULHWCH.

GOLL
In Irish Celtic mythology, Goll was the son of the king of Magh Mell and the nephew of FIACHNA. Goll abducted the wife of Fiachna and would not release her until Fiachna engaged the assistance of LAOGHAIRE MAC CRIMTHANN.

GOLL MAC MORNA
In Irish Celtic mythology, Goll mac Morna was the leader of the FIANNA before FIONN MAC CUMHAILL. He is said to have slain Cumhaill, Fionn's father, in order to gain leadership of the Fianna, and he is said to have later killed a son of Fionn's. Legend also has it that he married the daughter of Fionn. According to legend, he was present at the wedding feast of Fionn mac Cumhaill and GRAINNE and was one of those not drugged by Grainne when she went of with DIARMAID ua Duibhne.

GOOSE
To the Celts, the goose symbolized war and protection, and geese were sometimes buried with the dead bodies of warriors. The Celtic war-deities were sometimes depicted as being accompanied by geese.

GORBODUC

In British Celtic mythology, Gorboduc was a king of Britain who was supposed to be a descendant of BRUTUS. He was the husband of JUDON and the father of PORREX and FERREX. Porrex killed Ferrex, and Judon killed Porrex in a fit of grief at the loss of her son Ferrex. Thus when Gorboduc died there was no successor and the supposed line from Brutus died out.

GORIAS

In Irish Celtic mythology, Gorias was one of the four great cities of the TUATHA DE DANANN, the others being Falias, Finias and Murias. LUGH brought his invincible sword from Gorias.

GORLOIS *see* UTHR BENDRAGON.

GOSPELS, ILLUMINATED *see* ILLUMINATED GOSPELS.

GOWRA *see* GABHRA.

GRAIL

According to some sources, the cup that Jesus drank from at the Last Supper was known as the Holy Grail. According to other sources, the Holy Grail was the cup that was used to catch the blood from the wound inflicted by the centurion Longinus on Jesus as he hung upon the cross. JOSEPH OF ARIMATHEA is said to have arrived in Glastonbury in the first century AD. He is said to have brought the Holy Grail with him together with two bottles containing the blood and sweat of Jesus. The Grail was handed down from generation to generation and then became the centre of a quest that was central to the Arthurian saga, GALAHAD eventually finding it. However, the basis of the idea of a quest for some kind of vessel appears to have come from Celtic traditions. It may be connected with the journey to the OTHERWORLD to find a magical CAULDRON.

GRAINNE

In Irish Celtic mythology, Grainne was the beautiful daughter of CORMAC MAC AIRT, a high king. She became betrothed to FIONN MAC CUMHAILL when he was already old. One story has it that he saw her when she had been transformed into a deer and fell in love with her. Grainne was not keen on the idea of marriage to Fionn because of his age and because she was in love with DIARMAID ua Duibhne. During the wedding feast that took place the night she was due to marry Fionn, Grainne drugged most of the company and placed Diarmaid under a GEIS to elope with her to a wood in Connacht. Some of the company were left undrugged to act as witnesses to Diarmaid's promise.

They were pursued by Fionn and his FIANNA. Diarmaid kept leaving Fionn symbolic messages that he had not had sexual relations with Grainne. He refused to do so for a long time, until Grainne's derision finally got the better of him and he agreed to sleep with her. Fionn's pursuit lasted for many years, but at last OENGHUS intervened and managed to effect some form of reconciliation between Fionn and Grainne and Diarmaid. Grainne had four sons and a daughter by Diarmaid. However, the reconciliation was not really complete as Fionn still bore a grudge. When Diarmaid was mortally wounded by his foster brother, the boar BEANN GHULBAN, his only hope was to receive water from Fionn's hands. Twice Fionn let the water that might have saved his life slip through his fingers and by the time he was doing the same with the third lot Diarmaid was dead. According to one legend, Grainne at first swore vengeance and began to have her sons trained so that they could one day kill Fionn. Fionn, however, began to woo her, and she eventually agreed to be his bride.

GRANNOS
In Gaulish Celtic mythology, Grannos was a god of healing who possibly became assimilated with the classical god Apollo. He is often depicted in conjunction with SIRONA, who is regarded as being his consort.

GRONW PEBYR
In Welsh Celtic mythology, Gronw was the lover of BLODEUWEDD. Together they tried to kill her husband, LLEU LLAW GYFFES. This was easier said than done, because certain conditions had to be fulfilled before Lleu Llaw Gyffes could be killed. His wife knew this but not what the conditions were. However, she succeeded in getting her husband to tell her how he could be killed and even to demonstrate the rather odd stance in which he could be killed. Gronw then set about the task of killing Lleu. He succeeded in wounding him, and Lleu changed into an eagle and flew away to die of his wound. GWYDION FAB DON succeeded in healing his wound, and Lleu returned to kill Gronw. Blodeuwedd was transformed into an owl as a punishment for her infidelity and conspiracy to kill her husband.

GROVE

Although the Celts sometimes built temples for the worship
of their gods, they very often used natural landscape features
as the centre of their worship. Sacred groves were common
places of worship with the Celts, the DRUIDS being in charge
of this worship. Many TREES were sacred to the Celts, and a
group of these was regarded as being even more sacred.

GUNDESTRUP CAULDRON

One of the most impressive of all the Celtic relics that have
come to light is the Gundestrup Cauldron. It was found in
1891 in a bog at Vesthimmerland in Jutland by a man cutting
peat. Made of almost pure silver, it was probably originally
gilded and would have been a ceremonial vessel. It holds more
than twenty-eight gallons and consisted of a base plate and
five inner and seven outer panels. Before the CAULDRON was
buried, the silver panels had been dismantled. The panels appear to depict some kind of mythological narrative, with gods,
people and animals portrayed. Several of the figures are well-
known Celtic cult figures, such as CERNUNNOS, the stag-horned
god. One of the panels shows three bulls about to be slaughtered, while others show more exotic animals, such as lions,
leopards and elephants. Several goddesses are depicted, and
among these is a female deity flanked by WHEELS, as though
she were travelling in a cart. One of the panels depicts a pro-
cession of Celtic foot-soldiers and cavalry.

There is controversy about the date and origins of the cauldron. One suggestion is that it was made between the fourth
and third centuries BC and that it was made in Romania or

Thrace. It is thought to have been wrought by several silver-smiths. Although many of the symbols depicted are obviously Celtic in origin, many do not seem to have a parallel in the Celtic art of Western Europe. There is speculation that either craftsmen from southeast Europe made the cauldron for more northern Celts or else that the cauldron had been stolen from Gaul by Celtic invaders. It was quite usual for cauldrons and other artefacts to be buried in WATER as a votive offering. It also might have been hidden for safety.

GWALCHAFED *see* GALAHAD.

GWAWL FAB CLUD
In Welsh Celtic mythology, Gwawl fab Clud was the suitor whom RHIANNON rejected to marry PWYLL. He was determined still to marry her and tricked Pwyll on the wedding feast on the eve of his wedding to Rhiannon to grant him a favour. Pwyll, without thinking, agreed to the favour, not knowing who Gwawl was. When Gwawl revealed the nature of the favour, he had to accede to the request, even although this was to marry Rhiannon. For details of how Rhiannon succeeded in making sure that she married Pwyll after all, *see* PWYLL.

GWENDOLEN *see* HABREN.

GWERN
In Welsh Celtic mythology, Gwern was the son of BRANWEN and of MATHOLWCH, king of Ireland. The sovereignty of Ireland was bestowed on him to avoid battle between BENDIGEID VRAN and Matholwch. However, the boy was cast into a fire

by EFNISIEN, and the battle between Matholwch and Bendigeid Vran began.

GWION BACH
In Welsh Celtic mythology, Gwion was the son of GWREANG. According to legend, TALIESIN was Gwion reincarnate. When CERRIDWEN was making her potion to give her son AFAGDDU the gift of knowledge and wisdom, she chose Gwion to stir the potion. After stirring it for about a year, he got three drops of the potion on his finger and put it in his mouth to cool down. Cerridwen was furious and pursued him, both turning into various shapes, until Gwion became a grain of wheat on the threshing-barn floor and Cerridwen turned into a hen and ate him up. She then became pregnant, had a baby boy, put him in a leather bag and threw him in the river. He was found by ELFFIN, who named him Taliesin, which translates as 'radiant brow', because the boy was so beautiful.

GWREANG
In Welsh Celtic mythology, Gwreang was the father of GWION BACH, who became TALIESIN.

GWREIDAWL
In Welsh Celtic mythology, Gwreidawl was the father of Gwythyr. *See* GWYN AP NUDD.

GWRHRYR
In Welsh Celtic mythology, Gwrhryr was one of the party formed to help CULHWCH in his quest for OLWEN. Gwrhryr was chosen because he could interpret the language of animals and so could ask them for directions.

GWRI

In Welsh Celtic mythology, Gwri was the name given to PRYDERI by TEYRNON when the baby turned up on his doorstep.

GWYDDBWYLL *see* FIDCHELL.

GWYDION FAB DON

In Welsh Celtic mythology, Gwydion fab Don was a magician and a poet and the son of DON. He was the brother of GILFAETHWY and of ARANRHOD. He helped Gilfaethwy in his desire for GOEWIN by using his wiles and magic (*see also* MATH FAB MATHONWY). It was Gwydion who killed PRYDERI in single combat by using his magical powers.

GWYN AP NUDD

In Welsh Celtic mythology, Gwyn ap Nudd was a king of the OTHERWORLD. He abducted Creiddylad, even although she was engaged to be married to another man, Gwythyr, the son of Gwreidawl. It was agreed that Gwyn and Gwythyr should fight an annual combat and whoever won the combat that took place on doomsday would be the winner.

GWYN DUN MANE

In Welsh Celtic mythology, Gwyn Dun Mane was a cow that CULHWCH had to obtain for YSPADDADEN.

GWYN GOHOYN *see* PRYDERI.

GWYTHYR AP GWREIDAWL *see* GWYN AP NUDD.

H

HABREN

In British Celtic mythology, Habren was the daughter of Locrinus and his mistress, Estrildis. She and her mother were drowned as an act of vengeance by Gwendolen, the estranged wife of Locrinus, who had met his death in a battle against his wife. Gwendolen, although the cause of Habren's death, felt that the fact that Habren was Locrinus's daughter should not be forgotten and ordered that the river in which she was drowned should from then on bear the name of Habren. In Roman times the river was known as Sabrina and in modern times it is known as the River Severn.

HAFGAN

In Welsh Celtic mythology, Hafgan, whose name means 'summer white', was the rival and opponent of ARAWN, king of ANNW, with whom he is said to have taken part in an annual single combat contest. According to the legend, Hafgan was killed in combat not by Arawn but by PWYLL, lord of Dyfed. As a punishment for a hunting offence against Arawn, Pwyll had to take the form of Arawn for a year, during which time he had to meet Hafgan in the annual Hafgan/Arawn contest, with fatal results for Hafgan. Pwyll had been forewarned by Arawn that if Hafgan were to be killed this could be done only by a single blow because he had the magical ability of recovering from a blow if a second blow was administered. In the light of this knowledge, Pwyll refused to comply with the dying Hafgan's request to deliver a second blow, supposedly to put him out of his pain and misery but actually to allow him to revive.

HAG OF HELL
In Celtic mythology, the Hag of Hell was as a woman of supernatural powers who appears in the story of CULHWCH and OLWEN. To win the hand of Olwen in marriage, Culhwch had to complete a number of difficult tasks set by YSPADDADEN, father of Olwen. Obtaining the blood of the Hag of Hell was one of these tasks.

HALLOWEEN
Also known as All Hallows Eve, this is a festival still celebrated on the night of 31 October, now mainly by children. Traditionally it is associated with witches and warlocks, who are said to roam around freely then. It is the equivalent of the ancient Celtic festival of SAMHAIN, also celebrated on the night of 31 October, which in the old Celtic calendar marked the beginning of the year.

HALLSTATT
A village in Upper Austria, Hallstatt is situated by a lake in the region known as Salzkamergut, whose capital is Salzburg. Salzkamergut means 'the place of good salt' and Salzburg means 'salt town', indicating the importance of salt to the area. Salt is thought to have been mined at Hallstatt more

than two and a half thousand years ago, some of the early salt-miners having been Celts—the word *hall* is Celtic for salt. Austria is one of the oldest Celtic territories in Europe and the area around Hallstatt was one of the main Celtic settlements in Austria. There were important excavations in the second part of the nineteenth century (*see* HALLSTATT EXCAVATIONS) and Hallstatt has become not only a village famous for its Celtic connections but a term given to indicate a stage of development of Celtic culture and civilization wherever it was found (*see* HALLSTATT PERIOD).

HALLSTATT EXCAVATIONS

In 1846, George Ramsauer, the director of the Hallstatt State Salt Mine, discovered on a hill above the village of HALLSTATT a vast prehistoric cemetery situated under some curiously shaped grass-covered mounds. He conducted investigations on many of these ancient graves, which were about two and a half thousand in number, and the results of these investigations attracted the interest of the Academy of Sciences in Vienna. A team of professional investigators was sent from there to Hallstatt in 1876 and began exhaustive excavations in the area. Their discoveries put the Celts on the map, so to speak, since before that the ancient map of Europe had been dominated by the Greek and Roman civilizations. The Hallstatt excavations produced tangible evidence of another civilization whose people had a fixed habitation and were farmers and traders, reminding historians that the Greeks and Romans had referred to trade with a people who lived in areas of Central Europe and who were called KELTOI. The grave goods retrieved from the ancient cemetery at Hallstatt indicated that at that stage of their development the Celts were an iron-using people who had moved on from the Bronze Age. Many finely decorated vessels, weapons and horse trappings, all made of iron, were brought to the surface, as were pieces of leather clothing, shards of pottery, wooden utensils and dishes, and the remains of food. The excavations at Hallstatt have proved to be of immense importance in piecing together the culture of this ancient people, who were the Celts. So important were these excavations that the village gave its name to the HALLSTATT PERIOD or Hallstatt Culture, a means of assessing and indicating the stage of development of the civilization of the Celts generally.

HALLSTATT PERIOD *or* HALLSTATT CULTURE

These terms do not simply refer to the connection between the Celts and the Austrian village of HALLSTATT. Instead, they are used in standard archaeological parlance to indicate a means of assessing the stage of development and time span of Celtic civilizations, wherever these were situated geographically. The style of the artefacts excavated at the HALLSTATT EXCAVATIONS has been used as a standard by which to assess the age and level of development and sophistication of other Celtic settlements, the other major standard being referred to as the LA TÈNE CULTURE, named after a Swiss lakeside settlement. It is difficult to give exact dates in connection with things that happened so long ago, and there is some variation among historians of the dates that should be ascribed to the Hallstatt Period. Roughly speaking, it can be regarded as stretching from about 750 BC until about 450 BC.

HAMMER-GOD

One of the important Gaulish Celtic divinities was the Hammer-god. A representation of him has been found on many stone monuments and bronze figurines. He is usually depicted with a kind of hammer with a long shaft and a mallet-type head and a small vessel, such as a pot or goblet. Frequently he is represented as bearded and as wearing a short belted tunic and a heavy cloak. Sometimes he appears alone and sometimes he is part of a couple. The Hammer-god appears to have had several associations. He seems to have been connected with healing, as his statue frequently is situated at the sites of healing SPRINGS, and he was also in some parts of Gaul, such as Burgundy, associated with wine and grapes. He is also associated with the sun and with earthly prosperity.

HARP

The Irish harp is referred to extensively in Celtic myths and legends, and there are examples of it depicted on Celtic stone carvings dating from the eighth and ninth centuries in Ireland and in the west of Scotland. However, there are only fourteen surviving instruments and fragments of instruments from the whole of the early period during which the traditional form of the Irish harp flourished. The lack of concrete information is further exacerbated by the fact that the makers of the traditional Irish harps were not in the habit of either signing the instruments or dating them. What is known is that the Irish harps were of a heavier and bulkier construction than harps in other countries and, perhaps from the twelfth century, were strung with brass. There were two distinct forms of European harp by the fourteenth century, one being the sturdily built Irish harp and the other being a lighter, more delicate instrument commonly referred to as the Gothic or Romanesque harp. Legend has it that the harp came into being after a woman fell asleep on the seashore and heard the wind blowing through the sinews of the skeleton of a whale that was lying near her. On hearing her story, her husband made a wooden frame and equipped it with whale sinews to make the first harp. A less romantic account of the origins of the harp suggests that the instrument was brought to Ireland from Greece.

HEAD, THE

The head was particularly revered by the ancient Celtic peoples. To them it was much more important than the heart, which was revered by other civilizations. The Celts regarded the head as housing the soul and even seem to have believed that the head could function without the rest of the body. It is probably for that reason that the ancient Celts are said to have decapitated enemies killed in battle and carried the heads from the battlefield, often attached to the necks of their horses. They would then display the heads on posts outside their settlements or nail them up on their houses, as some hunters now hang up stags' heads as trophies. The greater the owner of the head had been, the more honour went to the Celtic warrior who displayed the head as a trophy. It is also said that the Celts sometimes preserved the heads of some of their more important foes by embalming them in cedar oil and storing them in chests. Evidence of the Celtic habit of severing heads and keeping them as trophies was discovered by the Romans when they defeated the Celtic tribe, the Salii. They found a sanctuary, constructed by the Salii at Entremont in Provence, that was dedicated to the cult of the severed head. There were examples of carved heads but they also found the remains of actual human heads. Human skulls and severed heads were also found in stone pillars at Roquepertuse in Bouches-du-Rhône.

The head, as befitting something that was of such importance to the Celts, features frequently in Celtic mythology. In one of the legends associated with CUCHULAINN, he is set upon by twelve enemy warriors but succeeds in defeating all of them at once and cuts off their heads. He then set up twelve stones in the ground and impaled one of the heads on each stone. Other legends demonstrate the supposed ability to function without its missing body. For example, in the Welsh legend of BENDIGEID VRAN, when Bendigeid is mortally wounded in his war against MATHOLWCH, the Irish king, he asks his followers to decapitate him and take his head back home from Ireland. During the long voyage back, his head, according to the legend, was able to eat, drink and talk, just as it had done when he was alive and it was attached to his body. In later more civilized times when the macabre practice of decapitation had been abandoned by the Celts, the cult of the head remained important to them. This is obvious from the many stone carvings of heads that have been discovered in the areas in which the Celts flourished. Some of these were located at sacred places, such as temples, shrines or sacred wells, as though the carved head was acting as a protector. The head was also used to decorate more everyday things. Various excavations have revealed buckets and bowls with representations of the human head acting as handles.

HEFEYDD HEN

Hefeydd in Welsh mythology was the father of RHIANNON, the wife of PWYLL. He was known as Hen, meaning 'old' or 'ancient', in view of his advanced years.

HEILYN

In Welsh Celtic mythology, Heilyn was one of only seven Britons who survived the terrible war in Ireland between MATHOLWCH and BENDIGEID VRAN. Heilyn is said to have opened the magic door through which the seven survivors escaped from the Island of Gwales, having spent eighty years there on their way back from Ireland after the war.

HEININ

In Welsh Celtic mythology, Heinin was the chief bard at the court of King ARTHUR at the time when TALIESIN arrived.

HELENA

In British mythology, Helena was the daughter of Coel, said to be the founder of Colchester. According to legend, she married Constantius Chlorus, the Roman emperor, after peace had been made between him and Coel following the three-year-old siege of Colchester by Constantius. Their son was Constantine the Great. Helena is identified with St Helena.

HELIG AP GLANNOWG

In Welsh Celtic mythology, Helig was the ruler of a kingdom

in the sixth century. It is said to have been situated about ten miles out to sea from Colwyn Bay. From the nineteenth century there have been claims of sightings of the ruins of Helig's palace.

HELVETII
The Helvetii were a Celtic tribe who tried to migrate across Gaul to establish settlements on the Atlantic coast, having been driven out of their settlements in what is now Germany. Julius Caesar feared that their presence would interfere with his plans for settling and controlling GAUL, and he and his army attacked and inflicted a terrible, bloody defeat on the Helvetii at Armecy.

HERNE THE HUNTER
In British Celtic mythology, Herne was the name of a giant with antlers on his head who was probably connected with the Celtic cult of CERNUNNOS. According to legend, Herne in modern times lives in Windsor Great Park.

HIR ATRYM AND HIR ERWN
Hir Atrym and Hir Erwn feature in the Welsh Celtic legend of CULHWCH and OLWEN. They were two brothers who had absolutely insatiable appetites. They could eat vast quantities of food that was provided for them and then they would lay bare the land around them as well.

HIGH CROSS
The Celtic high cross is a well-known part of Celtic culture, and there are several examples of these situated in Britain and Ireland, for example on IONA and ISLAY in Scotland, at

KILMALKEDAR in Ireland and Llantwit Major in Wales (*see* HOUELT CROSS). Some of these freestanding crosses are thought to be twelve hundred years old or more. The early high crosses were often quite plain and undecorated, but many of the later ones were richly carved. Such carvings include the knotwork typical of Celtic culture, spiral patterns or patterns consisting of raised bosses, the latter perhaps included as symbols of the sun, which was a source of worship for the early Celts. Other subjects for carving included animals or mythical beasts and biblical scenes. Celtic high crosses were often constructed to indicate a meeting place, perhaps within a monastery, rather than to indicate a burial place.

HILL FORT

In Britain in the Iron Age a favourite place of occupation of the Celts was the hill fort. Such a settlement enabled them to observe the land below and to look out for any approaching danger, such as a marauding army. Some of the hill forts occupied by the Celts predate their arrival in Britain. A number of the sites that the Celts used had been in existence since Neolithic times, and the Celts reinforced their security rather than starting them from scratch. Instead of using high wooden fences to keep the settlement livestock in and any invaders out, the Celts made huge earthen ramparts that can still be seen in some of the areas of Britain that they inhabited. Some of the finest of the Celtic hill forts are located in western and southern Britain, and a particularly fine example is Maiden Castle near Dorchester in Dorset. Consisting of a vast enclosed area of over forty acres, it is the largest Celtic hill fort dating from the Iron Age in Europe. Fortunately, a number of the Celtic hill forts are still in a good state of preservation today—another fine example being at Eggardon, situated at the extremity of a long chalk ridge that crosses the south of England, *don* or *dun* being Celtic for 'fort', and so the historian, both professional and amateur, is able to get quite a good idea of what the Celtic hill fort was actually like. The entrance to the hill fort, as can be seen clearly at Maiden Castle, was a labyrinth-like series of earthen ramparts designed both to confuse and repel any potential invaders, although they had little effect on the Roman army when it invaded Britain in AD 43. The hill forts were constructed near ready sources of water such as dew ponds. Security and defence were, of course, important aspects of the Celtic hill forts, but they were certainly not simply military settlements. The hill forts acted as a kind of general headquarters for the local tribe of the area, for peaceful as well as warlike purposes. They functioned also as religious centres, and the Roman invaders often continued to observe the religious associations of the hill forts after they had taken them over, perhaps afraid of the Celtic deities wreaking vengeance on them. In many cases the hill forts also functioned as centres where the Celtic craftsmen could practise their art and produce goods.

HILL SITES *or* TORS

The early people, including the Celts, often made use of hills in their religious ritual. The SUN often featured in their worship, and a hill was the perfect place from which to observe its rising and setting. The view of this would have been even more dramatic if the surrounding countryside were flat, and perhaps it is for this reason that the Celts and other early peoples were attracted to the hills or mounds that rise from the otherwise flat surrounding land in parts of the south of Britain. So important were such hills or mounds considered to be that some of them were man-made, notably the huge hill site at Silbury Hill in Wiltshire. This is the largest man-made hill site in western Europe and is said to be over four thousand years old. Some other hill sites were naturally occurring hills that had been amplified by man-made additions. Some of the hill sites connected with early religious ritual are surrounded by a kind of ridging or terracing, and various theories have been put forward to account for this. One theory suggest that the ridging marks the remains of a prehistoric processional maze by which the worshippers made their way to the top of the hill. Another theory suggests that the ridging is simply evidence of early agricultural methods. One of the best-known hill sites is GLASTONBURY TOR.

HOCHDORF

The village of Hochdorf is situated in southern Germany near the Black Forest. Its claim to fame in terms of the Celts lies in the fact that in the late 1970s a Celtic burial mound was discovered and investigated by Dr Jorg Biel, an archaeologist from Baden-Württemberg. The burial mound was found to conceal a vast burial chamber built for a Celtic prince thought to have been buried around 550 BC. The excavations at Hochdorf are important in the history of Celts because of the sheer scale of the findings and because of the state of preservation of these, the grave site showing no signs of having been robbed or vandalized. The Celts, as was the case with other ancient peoples, believed that a dead person had to be supplied with the necessities of life in the afterworld, and the excavators found not only evidence of these but the remains of an elaborate cart that had been buried with the prince. The things deemed necessary for the prince's afterlife, including domestic utensils, drinking horns and weapons and a large bronze cauldron for holding honey mead, together with the other grave goods and grave clothes and trappings, shed much light on the lifestyle of an important Celtic warrior of the period. Most importantly, the sumptuousness of the clothes and the quantity and nature of the gold jewellery and trappings provided for the body of the prince certainly emphasized that the Celts were not a simple unsophisticated, poverty-stricken people, at least if you were one of their aristocracy.

HOK-BRAZ

In the Celtic legends of the Gauls, Hok-Braz was a huge GIANT who dwelt on the coast of Brittany. He was a great danger to sailors as one of his habits was to swallow three-masted ships.

HOLY GRAIL *see* GRAIL.

HORNS

Many Celtic deities that otherwise had a human form were represented as having horns or antlers, whether these were of the BULL, GOAT, RAM or STAG variety. Early horned sculptures have been found, and Iron Age coins show representations of horned beings, while bucket mounts consisting of horned heads have also come to light. Horned deities were particularly popular among the Brigantes in Britain. Although most horned gods are represented as men, some dressed as warriors, female horned deities are portrayed at Icklingham in Suffolk and Richmond in Kent. Animals were extremely important in the Celtic culture and so perhaps this association between human deity and horn is not surprising. The horns are thought to have been symbolic of aggression, virility and fertility.

HORSES

As is obvious from the grave goods that have been retrieved from burial sites, the Celts were great horsemen and they used horse-drawn chariots to great effect in their battles against their foes. Their high regard for the horse is demonstrated by the effigies and carvings of horses that have been discovered at various Celtic sites throughout Europe, including the large-scale hillside horse carvings, often in chalk soil, of which the White Horse of Uffington near Oxford is a prime example. The horse was not held in regard by the Celts for its role in battle but for its associations with speed, beauty, sexual potency and fertility. Such was the importance of the horse in Celtic culture that horse sacrifices and ritual practices concerning dead horses were common. Some of the Iron Age burial sites were found to contain not only people, such as princes or charioteers, but CHARIOTS or wagons and horses, aids to the journey into the next world. The importance of the horse to the Celts is also manifested in their habit of representing deities on horseback. These mounted gods were often depicted in the guise of warriors. Some of the pre-Roman Celtic sanctuaries in southern Gaul were decorated with stone images of mounted warriors, and mounted warrior gods were particularly worshipped by the Catuvellauni and the Corieltauvi tribes of eastern Britain. The Celts in GAUL worshipped the horse goddess, EPONA, who may be identified with Edain Echraidhe in Ireland and RHIANNON in Wales. The image of Epona is found depicted on several hundred stones in what was Gaul. Epona also found favour with the Romans, and she was worshipped by them also, often being associated in Roman times with corn, fruit and, later, fertility.

HOUELT CROSS
Houelt Cross is an example of a Welsh Celtic HIGH CROSS. It is situated at Llantwit Major.

HOUSES
In lowland Britain in the Iron Age the most usual form of Celtic dwelling was the round house. These round houses were built round a central pole with a timber frame secured to vertical posts, radiating out from this. The walls were low and made from wattle and daub, and the roof was thatched. Groups of round houses were built together forming villages and were often accompanied by animal shelters and storerooms of a structure similar to that of the houses. Reconstructed Celtic round houses can be seen in the Welsh Folk Museum at St Fagans, near Cardiff.

HUGH

In Irish Celtic mythology, Hugh was one of the four children of LIR who were turned into swans and destined to stay in that shape for nine hundred years, by AOIFE (1). The latter was the second wife of Lir, and she was jealous of his four children by his previous wife, AOBH, her own sister. Hugh and his siblings were restored to human shape in the time of St PATRICK but died soon after that.

HUNTER-GOD

Hunting was extremely important to the Celts, as it was to all early peoples, this being the basis of their survival. Thus it is not surprising that the Celtic culture extends its range of deities to hunter-gods. These are distinguishable by their weapons and sometimes by their dress. For example, a hunter-god might be represented as carrying a bow and a quiver of arrows, often with a representation of a dog beside him. Although the purpose of a hunt is obviously to kill an animal, the hunter-gods appear to have been on the side of the hunted as well as the hunter. The hunter-gods are frequently depicted as being accompanied by live animals of the kind liable to be hunted, and they are sometimes represented as wearing HORNS, suggesting an affinity between hunter-god and animal of prey.

HWICCE

Hwicce was an ancient Celtic kingdom covering roughly the territory now covered by Gloucestershire and Worcestershire. Its capital was Deerhurst.

HWYCHDWN

In Welsh mythology, Hwychdwn was the son of the brothers GWYDION FAB DON and GILFAETHWY and the brother of HYDWN. Hwychdwn was born when the brothers were in the second year of their punishment in animal shape and so was born in the shape of a wild pig. He was turned into a human boy by MATH FAB MATHONWY, who had imposed the punishment on his parents.

HY-BREASAL or HY-BREASIL or HY-BRASIL

In Irish Celtic mythology, Hy-Breasal was an island off the west coast of Ireland that was visible above the water only once every seven years. According to legend, the island would rise to the surface of the water permanently if it came into contact with fire and would then become an earthly paradise. The island is said to have been ruled by Breasal. As with all legends, various forms of Celtic legends become confused with each other, and one legend has it that MANANNAN MAC LIR, the son of LIR, was responsible for the sinking of Hy-Breasal under the sea. Legend often also becomes confused with fact, although the fact is usually somewhat hazy. So it is that Hy-Breasal is recorded as having being a real place. When explorers travelled to South America and discovered Brazil, they thought that they had found Hy-Breasal, although early cartographers thought that it was in southwest Ireland, where legend had placed it.

HYDWN

In Welsh Celtic mythology, Hydwn was the son of the brothers GWYDION FAB DON and GILFAETHWY. He was born as a fawn because he was born during the time that Gwydion and Gilfaethwy had to spend in the shape of deer. The two brothers had been condemned by MATH FAB MATHONWY to spend three years in animal form, the first in the form of male and female deer, the second in the form of swine and the third in the form of wolves, for raping GOEWIN. It was another part of their punishment to produce an offspring at the end of each year in the animal shape that they then were in. The young fawn they gave birth to was changed into a human child by Math fab Mathonwy and named Hydwn. He had two brothers, HWYCHDWN and BLEDDYN.

I

IALONUS
In Gaulish Celtic mythology, Ialonus was a deity associated with cultivated fields. He is thought also to have been associated with glades, since *ialo* means 'glade'.

IANUARIA
In Gaulish Celtic mythology, Ianuaria was a female deity who was venerated at the sanctuary of Beire-le-Châtel in Burgundy. Very little is known about her history or associations, although a small stone statuette depicting a young girl with curly hair, thought to be a representation of the goddess, was found at the sanctuary. The statuette is clad in a pleated coat and is holding a set of pipes, and from this latter fact it has been deduced that Ianuaria might have been associated with music, although it might be assumed that her primary association was with healing, the sanctuary at Beire-le-Châtel being dedicated to healing.

IARBANEL
In Irish Celtic mythology, Iarbanel was said to have been the ancestor of the TUATHA DE DANANN. He was one of the three sons of NEMEDH who succeeded in escaping after the defeat and death of their father.

IATH N' ANANN

This was an ancient name for Ireland and may be derived from *Anu* or *Ana*, an alternative form of DANU, a MOTHER-GODDESS.

IBERIA

The Celts are thought to have had extensive settlements in Iberia, which consists of Spain and Portugal, perhaps from as early as 900 BC. According to Irish legend, the Celts who colonized Ireland came from Spain. The Celts in Iberia became involved in the war between Carthage and Rome and paid a heavy price for this involvement. The Carthaginian general Hamilcar Barca invaded the southern coast of Iberia and his son, Hannibal, decided to launch an attack on Rome through the territory of the Celts. The Celts formed an alliance with Hannibal and the Romans took their revenge on them after the fall of Carthage in 197 BC. The Romans conquered and colonized the Iberian Celts and often treated them extremely savagely. Servius Sulpicius Galba even massacred the Celts after they had surrendered in 151 BC. War between the Celts and Romans in Iberia continued until the middle of the first century BC. After that the Celts seem gradually to have become assimilated into the Roman way of life.

IBHELL

In Irish mythology, Ibhell was the beautiful wife of Aed, the son of the king of Connacht. The king of Leinster fell in love with her, and MONGAN used this as a way of taking revenge on the king of Leinster who had abducted Mongan's wife. He used his skill as a magician to adopt the form of Aed and transformed an ugly old hag into the form of Ibhell. The king of Leinster agreed to exchange Mongan's wife for the fake Ibhell, not of course realizing that this was a fake. He realized his error when the hag resumed her own form.

ICENI

The Iceni were an ancient British tribe and one of the leading tribes of the East Anglian area. It is particularly famous for one its queens, BOUDICCA. She was the wife of PRASUTAGUS. The Iceni allied themselves with the TRINOVANTES to mount attacks against the Roman invaders under the leadership of Boudicca and had three notable victories before being routed by the Romans.

ICOVELLAUNA

In Gaulish Celtic mythology, Icovellauna was a deity who was worshipped in the area around Metz and Trier. She is said to have presided over the healing SPRING of Sablon at Metz and is therefore associated with healing. No representations of the goddess have been uncovered.

IDRIS

In Welsh Celtic mythology, Idris was a GIANT who is said to have been skilled in poetry, astronomy and philosophy. His home was on the mountain of Cadair Idris in Gwynedd.

ILLAN *or* ULLAN

In Irish Celtic mythology, Illan was the husband of TUIREANN, described as either the sister or sister-in-law of FIONN MAC CUMHAILL. Illan had an affair with a druidess who became extremely jealous of his wife and changed Tuireann into a female wolfhound. Tuireann was pregnant at the time of her unfortunate transformation, and gave birth in her new shape.

Thus her sons, SGEOLAN and BRAN, were born as wolfhounds and later became the two famous hounds of Fionn. Following Illan's promise to desert his wife for her, the druidess changed Tuireann back into human form. Illan is also depicted as a king of Leinster who was thought to have led raids into Britain.

ILLUMINATED GOSPELS

These gospels, colourfully, intricately and painstakingly decorated by Celtic monks over a long period of time, are rightly considered to be one of the most important legacies that the Celtic culture has given us and indeed are considered a major contribution to the art world generally. The monks, of course, used only natural pigments to produce their brilliant blues, greens, yellows, and so on. The three finest extant examples are respectively the Book of KELLS and the gospel books of Lindisfarne and Durrow.

IMBAS FOROSNAI

In Irish Celtic mythology, this was a rite based on the fact that knowledge and sagacity could be imparted to someone who chewed the raw flesh of the thumb. FIONN MAC CUMHAILL is said to have done this after he had burned his thumb while cooking the SALMON OF KNOWLEDGE or wisdom and thus to have acquired his knowledge and wisdom.

IMBOLC *or* IMBOLG

This was one of the four Celtic festivals, the others being SAMHAIN, BELTANE and LUGHNASADH. It was celebrated on 1 February. It is associated with the lactation of ewes. The festival was also associated with the Irish goddess BRIGID. Subsequently this pagan festival was taken over by the Christian church as one of their festivals, the feast day of St Brigid.

IMMORTALITY

The Celts believed in the immortality of the soul and they were one of the first European people to hold such a belief. It was not a theory of reincarnation but a belief based on the fact that when a person died he or she simply changed places or worlds. This was why the Celts put not only bodies in graves but all the appurtenances necessary to sustain life, the notion being that the person would need all of this in the OTHERWORLD. The Celts seem to have believed in an constant exchange of souls taking place between this world and the Otherworld. Because they believed not only that a death in this world was the means of sending a soul to the Otherworld but that a death in the Otherworld was the means of bringing a soul to this world, the Celts are said to have mourned birth and celebrated death.

IMMRAM

This was the name given to the two main classifications of ancient Irish literature, the other being ECHTRAI. Immram referred to a tale concerning a long voyage, usually a fantastic voyage to an island kingdom, whether this was inhabited by humans or supernatural beings. The echtrai referred to a tale involving a journey made by a human or humans to a supernatural land either by crossing many tracts of water or by gaining entrance through a SIDH or burial mound.

INFANT BURIAL

There is some evidence of rituals involving dead babies in

the Celtic culture, although whether the babies all died naturally or whether some were the result of human SACRIFICE is not known. It is thought that interred infants may have been regarded as a means of propitiating the gods or as a means of conferring a blessing. Certainly it has been ascertained that the corpses of babies were included in the foundations of shrines and sanctuaries. At a shrine in Cambridge, dead babies were buried wearing shoes that were several sizes too big for them, perhaps because it was felt that the babies would go on growing in the OTHERWORLD.

INGCEL

In Irish Celtic legend, Ingcel was a monster with a single eye that contained three pupils, and he is said to have been the son of the king of Britain. He went into exile in Ireland and joined forces with the foster brothers of CONAIRE MOR, the high king, and some other dissidents. They made plundering raids in Ireland and Britain and killed Ingcel's father, mother and brothers. Ingcel and the band of marauders attacked DA DERGA'S HOSTEL and in the attack Conaire was killed, Conaire having ignored many prophecies of doom in order to travel there.

INTERPRETATIO CELTICA

This is a term used to describe the fusion of the Celtic and Roman religious cults. As a result of this fusion, Roman gods to some extent were accepted into the Celts' own set of beliefs. Roman gods were sometimes given a Celtic title also, such as Jupiter TARANIS. The converse of this process by which the Romans regarded some of the Celtic gods as part of the Roman culture—for example, the Romans named the Celtic goddess

S<small>ULIS</small> of Bath Sulis Minerva by a hybridization process—is known as *interpretatio romana*, a term that was used by Tacitus.

INTERPRETATIO ROMANA *see* INTERPRETATIO CELTICA.

INVASIONS, BOOK OF *see* L<small>EABHAR</small> G<small>ABHALA</small> E<small>IREANN</small>.

IONA

St Columba, or Columcille as he is known in Gaelic, established a Celtic Christian community at the Hebridean island of Iona, having travelled there as a missionary from Ireland in AD 563. The community dwelt in 'beehive huts', the remains of some of which can be seen on the island today. It is hardly surprising, then, that Iona is rich in tangible evidence of its association with the Celts and Celtic Christianity. There is much of interest there to anyone interested in the history of the Celts. Notably it is rich in Celtic HIGH CROSSES, although history suggests that there were originally many more but that most of these were destroyed by the Vikings who invaded the island from around the seventh century AD. There are today three fine examples of freestanding crosses. One is St Martin's Cross, which dates from the ninth century AD and stands five metres in height. It has various biblical scenes carved on the front of the cross, which is made of a hard volcanic stone. The back of the cross is richly carved with 'boss and serpent designs', the serpents probably pointing to a pagan influence incorporated into Christian art and worship. Another example of a freestanding Celtic cross on Iona is St John's Cross, which is situated outside the west door of the abbey. It is in fact a cast of the original cross, which dates from the late eighth century AD and has been removed for preservation and repair. Another high cross on the island is of a later date than the other two. It is McLean's Cross, which is a disc-headed crucifixion cross, having a carving depicting the Crucifixion in the centre of the round head. Tall and extremely slender, the high cross has carved panels of intricate design stretching right down the shaft.

It is not only high crosses for which Iona is noted in Celtic history. The island is also the site of the Well of Healing. Situated close to the summit of Dun-I, a granite outcrop about ninety metres in height, it takes the form of a large cleft in the rock filled with extremely cold water. Dedicated to St Columba, the well is thought to have been in use during his lifetime. Pilgrims seeking a cure from the well would climb to it if their disability allowed. Otherwise, water from it would be brought down to them.

Iona is not only associated with the Celts from the time of Columba. It has earlier Celtic connections with the DRUIDS. Indeed, the early Gaelic name for Iona was Innis na Druineach, which translates as the Isle of the Druids. There is today a thriving religious community on Iona, founded in the 1930s by Dr George MacLeod on the site of the Benedictine Abbey that was built in the Middle Ages over the foundations of Columba's original monastic settlement.

IRISH HARP *see* HARP.

IRNAN

In Irish Celtic legend, Irnan was one of the three sorceress daughters of Conaran who were sent by their father to capture some members of the FIANNA by spinning a magic web round them. GOLL MAC MORNA killed Irnan's sisters but spared her on condition that she released her captives. Irnan then changed into a monster and challenged FIONN MAC CUMHAILL or one of his warriors to face her in single combat as an act of vengeance for her sisters' death. Goll took Fionn's place and killed Irnan.

IRUSAN

In Irish Celtic mythology, Irusan was a huge cat that inhabited a cave near Knowth on the Boyne. The cat is said to have seized Seanchan Torpeist, the chief bard of Ireland, and to have run off with him.

ISLAY

The Scottish Hebridean island of Islay is rich in evidence of Celtic culture from the megalithic and early Christian periods. A particularly good example of this is sited at Kildalton, where a well-preserved early Celtic WHEEL cross dating from around AD 800 is located. The cross is about 2.7 metres in height and has carved on it in high relief an example of the 'nest of eggs' symbol, which appears also on St John's Cross on IONA. The significance of this symbol can only be speculated on. It has been suggested that it may be a symbol relating to the DRUIDS' worship of the SUN or nature. Another suggestion is that it denotes the Holy Trinity, but its true nature is lost in the mists of time. Another fine example of the Celtic craftsmanship is to be found on Islay at Kilnaver. This is the site of a Celtic HIGH CROSS 2.6 metres high and dating from around AD 850. The carvings on it, although difficult to make out, bear a resemblance to those on the high cross at KELLS in

County Meath in Ireland. At Kilchonan, also on Islay, is a fine example of a freestanding disc-headed cross, dating from around the late fourteenth century, and examples of some elaborately carved grave slabs. Islay is supposed to have had connections with St Columba (*see* IONA). According to tradition, his tutor in Ireland, St Ciaran, settled in the Rhinns of Islay and died there in AD 548.

ISLE OF MAN
There were Irish Celtic missionaries in the Isle of Man from the fifth century AD onwards, and Celtic carvings, such as the eighth-century Calf of Man Crucifixion slab, testify to their presence. However, the island was more heavily influenced by the Vikings who invaded and occupied it in the tenth century. An interesting piece of hybridization took place between Celtic and Viking culture. Sculptures were created by the Vikings that incorporated the Celtic HIGH CROSS framework and some of the symbols and patterns associated with these, such as knotwork, but also incorporated representations of characters from Norse sagas and Scandinavian runes.

ITH
In Irish Celtic legend, Ith was one of the Sons of MIL ESPAINE, who were the first human rulers of Ireland. As the name suggests, these invaders are supposed to have come from Spain and legend has it that Ith caught sight of Ireland from the top of a Spanish tower and set out to visit it. At first he was welcomed by the TUATHA DE DANANN, and he was invited by them to act as umpire and decide on the right to rule of MAC CUILL, MAC CECHT and MAC GREINE. He was so enthusiastic about

Ireland, however, that they began to suspect that he planned to take over the realm and so they killed him. His body was taken back to Spain, and a second Spanish expedition left for Ireland and conquered the Tuatha De Danann, making humans the rulers of Ireland.

ITINERARIUM CAMBRIAE

The Norman-Welsh chronicler and cleric, Giraldus Cambrensis (*c.*1146–*c.*1223) wrote *Itinerarium Cambriae* after he had journeyed through Wales in 1188 with the archbishop of Canterbury. It is an important source book of Welsh legend as the author recorded everything he was told by the local people, however unlikely.

ITALY

In the fourth century BC, the Celts expanded their area of settlement from GAUL to Italy. They were a warlike nation and around 390 BC they invaded Rome. The Romans were, however, to get their revenge in the second and first centuries BC when they moved into Gaul and forced the Celts to move north.

IUBDAN

In Irish Celtic legend, Iubdan was the elfin king of FAYLINN and husband of Queen BEBO. He and his wife visited the realm of Ulster to see the humans who dwelt there, having been put under a bond by EISIRT, his bard, to do so. Iubdan did not really believe that there was a giant people more powerful than his own. Iubdan and Bebo tried to slip into the palace of the king of Ulster, Fergus mac Leda, at night but were seized and held captive by Fergus. Despite a series of plagues imposed on Ulster by Eisirt and the people of Faylinn, Fergus refused to let the elfin couple go until he was presented with some of the magical treasures of Faylinn, such as a HARP that played by itself and shoes that enabled the wearer to walk on water. As with most legends, there are variations on the theme.

IUCHAR
In Irish Celtic legend, Iuchar was the son of TUIRENN and the brother of Brian and Iucharba. The three brothers killed CIAN whose son LUGH decided to take vengeance on them. He made the brothers collect a number of magical items that were required by the TUATHA DE DANANN for the Second Battle of MAGH TUIREDH. They completed the tasks but later died from injuries that they sustained when accomplishing the final task.

IUCHARBA
In Irish Celtic legend, Iucharba was the son of TUIRENN and the brother of Brian and IUCHAR.

IORUAIDHE
In Irish Celtic mythology, Ioruaidhe was a kingdom, the ruler of which was the owner of a hound that could not be defeated in a fight. It could catch any wild beast that it came across and it could turn to wine any water that it bathed in. Capturing this hound and taking it to Ireland was one of the tasks imposed on the sons of TUIRENN as a punishment for having killed CIAN. The brothers took the king of Ioruaidhe captive and offered to let him go free only on condition that they were given the hound.

IWERIADD *see* PENARDUN.

J

JOSEPH OF ARIMATHEA

According to legend, Christianity reached Britain with the arrival of Joseph Arimathea, said to be the uncle of Jesus, in the first century AD. He is supposed to have brought with him the cup that was used at the Last Supper and this was later known as the Holy GRAIL, becoming the subject of several quests. Joseph is said to have founded a Christian settlement at Glastonbury and to have buried the cup from the Last Supper there. The holy thorn tree there is said to have grown as a result of Joseph's planting his staff in the ground.

JUDON

In British Celtic mythology, Judon was the wife of GORBODUC, a king of Britain who was said to be a descendant of BRUTUS. She was the mother of two sons, FERREX and PORREX. Ferrex was killed by his brother and Judon then murdered Porrex. Judon and Gorboduc had no other children and neither of their dead sons had heirs, so the line of descent from Brutus died out.

JUPITER

The Roman god was adopted by the Celts into their own cult. He was often given a Celtic epithet, as Jupiter Taranis, TARANIS being the Celtic thunder-god.

K

KAMBER
In British Celtic mythology, Kamber was the son of BRUTUS and brother of LOCRINUS and Albanactus. After his father died, he became king of Wales, Locrinus became king of England and Albanactus became king of Scotland. Kamber helped Locrinus to defeat the Huns after they had killed Albanactus.

KELLS, BOOK OF
Celtic Christianity is associated with beautifully executed IL-LUMINATED GOSPELS, painstakingly crafted by Celtic monks. The best-known of these is the Book of Kells, which is located in the library of Trinity College in Dublin, it having been presented to the college during Cromwell's reign. The Book of Kells takes its name from an early monastery of this name in County Meath. According to tradition, the Book of Kells was executed on IONA and was taken to the monastery of Kells for preservation from the raids of the Vikings, but the first actual written reference to it is in the *Annals of Ulster* for 1006. There reference is made to it having been stolen from the monastery and retrieved after several months with the gold removed from it. It dates from the late eighth century AD and is profusely decorated with symbols relating not only to the

Celts, such as the famous KNOTWORK, but to the PICTS and the
Anglo-Saxons, with some evidence also of a Byzantine influence. Like other illuminated manuscripts, the Book of Kells
has been illustrated with highly coloured, naturally occurring
pigments, chiefly blue, green, yellow and red-brown. It is considered to be one of the finest legacies of the Celts.

KELTOI

The Greeks and Romans gave the name of Keltoi to the northern tribes of barbarians who threatened them from parts of
western and central Europe. The word may be the origin of
the word Celt.

KEY

Several representations of Celtic goddesses feature a key. It
is thought that the key may be symbolic of the ability of a
particular goddess to open the gates that lead to the
OTHERWORLD and so allow those who worship her to pass from
one life to another.

KILDALTON CROSS *see* ISLAY.

KILLARAUS

In Irish Celtic legend, this is the mountain in County Kildare
from which MYRDDIN transported the ring of stones known as
the GIANT'S RING. He is said to have re-erected this at STONE-
HENGE.

KILCHONAN *see* ISLAY.

KILMALKEDAR

An unusual Celtic cross is located in a churchyard at Kilmalkedar on the Dingle Peninsula in Kerry in Ireland. The top of the cross is in the form of a squared head and is called the Sundial Cross, it having been thought to have acted as a primitive sundial. It dates from the late seventh or early eighth century.

KNIGHTS

The idea of elite groups of warriors was part of Irish Celtic legend before King ARTHUR and his Knights of the Round Table came on the scene. The FIANNA were the members of an elite bodyguard who guarded the high kings of Ireland, founded in 300 BC by Fiachadh, the high king. There was also an Ulster military elite called the RED BRANCH, whose greatest champion was CUCHULAINN. This group of warriors was founded by ROSS THE RED of Ulster.

KNOTWORK

This is one of the most common designs on Celtic crosses and other forms of sculpture. As the name suggests, it involved designs based on knots.

L

LABHRAIDH LOINGSECH

In Irish Celtic mythology and originally named Maon or Moen (meaning 'dumb'), Labhraidh Loingsech was a king of Leinster who is supposed to have reigned around 268 BC. Legend has it that he was driven into exile by COBTHACH COEL, who made him devour part of his father's heart and part of his grandfather's heart. He was also forced to consume a mouse and her litter of young and then lost his voice. He rallied his men round him in Gaul and with the help of the men of Munster, under their ruler, SCORIATH, he reclaimed his lost kingdom. Pretending to make peace with his enemy, he invited Cobthach Coel and his followers to his court as his guests. They were given an iron chamber to rest in and their host lit a fire under it and burned them to death (*see also* LLASSAR LLAESGYNEWID). Labhraidh Loingsech is said to have had his speech restored by CRAFTINY's magic harp. As with other legends, there are some variations, and some say that it was the love of Moriath, daughter of Scoriath, that restored his voice. Moriath became Labhraidh's wife.

Another legend about Labhraidh Loingsech concerns his ears. In fact, he had horse's ears but this fact was unknown to everyone but his barber who cut his hair once a year. A

DRUID advised the barber to tell his secret to a tree, by which means he could share his secret but still keep it secret. However, the tree was cut down to make a harp, and the first time the harp was played in court by Craftiny it revealed the truth about the king's ears. Labhraidh Loingsech then admitted to the truth.

LABRAID LUATHLAM AR CLEB
In Irish Celtic mythology, Labraid Luathlam ar Cleb was the ruler of Magh Mell and husband of LI BAN.

LADRA
In Irish Celtic mythology, Ladra was the pilot who guided the ship of CESAIR on its voyage to Ireland. One of only three men on an expedition that had fifty women in it, legend has it that he argued with Cesair about the way in which the country should be divided up and went away to set up his own kingdom. With so many women and so few men around, Ladra is said to have indulged in so much sexual activity that he died of sexual excess.

LAEG *or* LOEG
In Irish Celtic mythology, Laeg was charioteer to CUCHULAINN, charioteers being important figures in Celtic culture. He is said to have been with Cuchulainn during his final battle with Erc and to have thrown himself in front of a spear thrown at his master, although Cuchulainn met his doom in the battle.

LAIGHIN (1)
Galian was renamed Laighin before it became LEINSTER. One suggestion as to why it was so named is that it was named

after the Gauls who went to Ireland with LABHRAIDH LOINGSECH to recover his kingdom.

LAIGHIN (2)

In Irish Celtic mythology, the name Laighin is also applied to the GAILIOIN, one of the three companies who came from Greece and invaded Ireland. They named themselves Laighin because they settled in Leinster.

LAIRGNEN

In Irish Celtic legend, Lairgnen was the son of a chief of Connacht. He was engaged to be married to DEOCA, who asked him to capture four famous singing swans as a wedding present. This he did, but the swans were in fact the children of LIR, who had been condemned to live as swans by AOIFE (1). Unfortunately for Lairgnen, just as he captured the beautiful swans they changed back into aged humans, their long period of penance being over.

LAKES

WATER was important in Celtic culture, and lakes held a particular significance. They were regarded as holy places through which gods could be reached. Many treasures, such as spears, swords, shields, brooches, horse and vehicle fittings, tools and CAULDRONS were deposited in these sacred lakes, there being archaeological evidence for this in the sites that have been excavated. For example, at the LA TÈNE site in Switzerland treasures were retrieved from a bay at the eastern end of Lake Neuchâtel.

LANHERNE CRUCIFIXION CROSS

A number of freestanding crosses can be found in Cornwall, the Cornish cross being shorter and squatter than those of Ireland, Scotland and Wales. One of the best examples of the Cornish Celtic cross is the Lanherne Crucifixion Cross, which dates from the tenth century AD. It has a pattern of interlacing and is dedicated to someone called Runhol, who may or may not have been the sculptor.

LAOGHAIRE

In Irish Celtic legend, there are several people of the name Laoghaire. One of these was a historical king of Ireland who was on the throne at the time that St PATRICK arrived in Ireland. Laoghaire and his followers were pagan and St Patrick was, of course, Christian. Having been brought by the druids before the king, St Patrick challenged Laoghaire to a contest to see which of their gods was the more powerful. The legend, according to Christian sources, indicates that two huts were set on fire as part of this contest. In one of these huts was put a druid wearing St Patrick's cloak and in the other was put a Christian young man wearing a robe belonging to a magician of the royal court. After the fire, it was discovered that the Christian youth was unharmed by the fire but the royal magician's robe had been completely burnt. It was also discovered that, while St Patrick's cloak was intact, the druid who had been wearing it had been burnt to death.

LAOGHAIRE BUADHACH *see* BRICRIU; CUCHULAINN.

LAOGHAIRE LORC *see* UGAINE MOR.

LAOGHAIRE MAC CRIMTHANN

In Irish Celtic legend, another of the name Laoghaire was Laoghaire mac Crimthann of Connacht. He assisted FIACHNA MAC RETACH in the task of regaining his wife and daughter, who had been abducted by GOLL of Magh Mell. He put Goll to death and married Der Greine, one of Fiachna's daughters.

LA TÈNE

A few kilometres outside Neuchâtel in Switzerland is located La Tène. In 1858, following unusually low water levels in the lake, were uncovered remains that were to be categorized as belonging to the second great period of Celtic culture, as HALLSTATT was the first. As was the case with Hallstatt, La Tène became a standard archaeological method of categorizing the stages of Celtic culture. La Tène Period or La Tène Culture represents Celtic civilization at the time of its maximum development from about the fifth century BC until the time of the Roman occupation. The artefacts found at La Tène were considerably more delicate, more sophisticated and more indicative of wealth and power than those of the Hallstatt Culture, showing that the Celts had moved on.

LEABHAR GABHALA EIREANN

This is a book dealing with the various mythological invasions of Ireland and as such is a mythical history of Ireland, being also known as the *Book of Invasions*. It survived in various ancient forms, principally in the form of the *Book of Leinster*, dating from the twelfth century. A version of the book was compiled from several ancient manuscripts now no longer extant by Micheal O Cleirigh (*c.*1575–*c.*1645). When

the *Book of Invasions* is referred to, it is usually this transla-
tion that is meant. The invasions dealt with in the book include the pre-Flood journey by CESAIR. It also includes the
invasion of PARTHOLAN, who, with his followers, defeated the
FOMORII, a race of half-human monsters, and the invasion of
NEMEDH, after whose death the Fomorii returned. The next
invasion dealt with is that of the FIR BHOLG, who were accompanied by the GAILIOIN and the Fir Dhomhnann, all three
of these tribes being the descendants of the Nemedh. The fifth
invasion mentioned is that of the TUATHA DE DANANN, also
descended from the Nemedh, and the sixth is that of the
Milesians or the Sons of MIL ESPAINE who defeated the Tuatha
De Danann. Eventually the two sides worked out an agree-
ment by which the Milesians ruled the part of the land above
ground and the Tuatha De Danann ruled the underground part.

LEINSTER

In Irish Celtic mythology, Leinster was one of the five provinces into which the FIR BHOLG divided Ireland. *See* LAIGHIN.

LIA

In Irish Celtic mythology, Lia was lord of Luachar in Connacht. He was treasurer of the FIANNA and keeper of the he-
reditary treasures that had passed to them from the TUATHA
DE DANANN. He was killed by FIONN MAC CUMHAILL who took
the bag of treasure.

LI BAN

In Irish Celtic mythology, Li Ban was the wife of LABRAID
LUATHLAM AR CLEB and sister of FAND. She invited CUCHULAINN

to help slay three FOMORII, promising him Fand as a lover in return.

LIMB VOTIVE
It was a custom of the Celts to present models of diseased limbs to deities at the various healing shrines and sanctuaries. Sometimes these were in wood and sometimes they were in stone. Models of organs other than arms or legs, such as breasts, heads, eyes and internal organs, were also presented. The idea obviously was that if a votive limb or other organ was given to a god or goddess then he or she would cure the actual limb or organ of any disease. Evidence of the practice of limb or organ votives has been found at various excavated sites. The offering of models of limbs and organs to deities for healing purposes was not confined to the Celts, it being found in various other early cultures.

LINDISFARNE *see* ILLUMINATED GOSPELS.

LINDOW MAN
In August 1984 part of a human body was uncovered in a peat bog at Lindow Moss in Cheshire. The body was that of a young man and it was face down in a crouching position and painted in different colours. He was naked apart from an armlet of fur. The young man, who became know as Lindow Man, had probably been placed in the bog around the fourth century BC. Lindow Man is thought to be evidence of the Celtic practice of human SACRIFICE. He had been hit on the head and garotted, and he looked as though he had been pushed from the back into the bog. His stomach contents revealed the presence of

mistletoe pollen, suggesting that the young man may have featured in some form of DRUID sacrifice. *See* TOLLUND MAN.

LINNE *see* OSCAR.

LIR

In Irish Celtic mythology, Lir was the sea-god, the equivalent of the Welsh god LLYR. He was the father of MANANNAN who became in turn the sea-god. He married AOBH and the children whom he had by her were turned into swans for nine hundred years by AOIFE (1), his second wife, because she was jealous of Lir's love for them.

LLASSAR LLAESGYNEWID

In Welsh Celtic mythology, Llassar Llaesgynewid was the husband of Cymidei Cymeinfoll, who gave birth once every six weeks not to a baby but to a fully grown clad, armed warrior. They created havoc in their native Ireland, and MATHOLWCH planned to get rid of them. He built an iron house and got the whole family to go into it and lit fires around it to roast those inside (*see also* LABRAIDH LOINGSECH). The children perished, but the parents escaped and went to Wales. They took with them a CAULDRON that had the power to heal warriors who had been wounded if they were cast into it. It also had the power to bring back to life dead warriors.

LLEFELYS

In Welsh Celtic mythology, Llefelys was the son of BELI and brother of LLUDD. He was the ruler of Gaul and helped his brother, who was ruler of Britain, to get rid of the three plagues.

LLEU LLAW GYFFES

In Welsh Celtic mythology, Lleu Llaw Gyffes was a warrior god who may have some form of association with the Irish god LUGH. His mother, ARANRHOD, was annoyed when he was born because she was hoping to get a post as foot-holder at the court of MATH FAB MATHONWY, a post that could be held only by a virgin. She placed three taboos on the boy at his birth. The first was that he should receive no name until his mother chose to give him one, the second was that he should never bear arms unless he was equipped with these by his mother, and the third was that he would never marry a human woman.

The brother of Aranrhod was GWYDION, the magician, who concealed the baby at birth and adopted him. He then set about undoing the taboos. First, by disguising himself and the boy, he tricked Aranrhod into naming the boy Lleu Llaw Gyffes, which means 'the bright one of the skilful hand'. Later he tricked her into arming the boy by pretending that her castle was under attack and in need of defending. He solved the marriage problem by enlisting the help of Math. Together they fashioned a woman out of flowers and named her BLODEUWEDD. Lleu married her, but they did not live happily ever after. Blodeuwedd had an affair with GRONW PEBYR, and she and her lover planned to kill her husband. Lleu was difficult to kill, as various conditions had to be met before this could happen, these conditions varying from one version of the legend to another. One says that Lleu had to have one foot on the edge of a vat of water and the other on a goat's back before he could be slain. An embellishment suggests that he could be killed in this position only by a

140

spear that had been worked on for a year and a day at Mass time on Sundays. However, Blodeuwedd succeeded in getting him to reveal how he might be killed and reported back to her lover. She persuaded Lleu to adopt the position, saying that she wanted to see what it looked like. The unsuspecting Lleu did so and was pierced through by Gronw with a spear that he had made under the specified conditions. Lleu was only injured, turned into an eagle and escaped to an OAK tree where Gwydion tracked him down and healed him. He turned him back into a human and Lleu then killed Gronw. Blodeuwedd was punished by being turned into an owl.

LLUDD

In Welsh Celtic mythology, Lludd was the son of Beli and the brother of LLEFELYS. He ruled Britain while Llefelys ruled GAUL, and during that time three plagues beset Britain. One of these was a demoniac race called the CORANAID, who could hear anything anyone whispered if the winds caught the whisper. The two brothers slew them with insects to which ordinary people were immune. Another of the plagues was a scream that occurred every May Day eve and the source of which could not be located. Llefelys discovered that the scream came from two fighting dragons and arranged for them to be captured in an underground chamber beneath Dinas Emrys. The third plague was a giant wizard. He was defeated in single combat by Lludd.

LLUDD LLAW EREINT

In Welsh Celtic mythology, Lludd Llaw Ereint was the equivalent of NUADA. He was the father of Creiddylad, and it has

141

been suggested that she was the original of Cordelia, the daughter of King Lear. He is sometimes confused with LLUDD, and sometimes their legends are run together.

LLWYD
In Welsh Celtic mythology, Llwyd was the son of Cil Coed and the friend of GWAWL. To avenge PWYLL's treatment of Gwawl, Llwyd put a curse on the Dyfed and took RHIANNON and her son PRYDERI prisoner. They were rescued by MANAWYDAN.

LLYN CERRIG BACH
A LAKE on the island of Anglesey that was sacred to the Celts was Llyn Cerrig Bach. Metal votive gifts dating from between the second century BC and the first century AD have been recovered. Many of these are associated with warfare and the aristocracy, suggesting that Celtic chiefs travelled to it to present votive gifts.

LLYCHLYN
In Welsh Celtic legend, Llychlyn was the name for Scandinavia or Norway , meaning 'land of lakes'. It is the equivalent of the Irish Lochlann. It has also been suggested that it was a name for the OTHERWORLD.

LLYR
In Welsh Celtic mythology, Llyr was cognate with the Irish god LIR. He is thought to have been the original of Shakespeare's King Lear.

LLYN-Y-FAN FACH
In Welsh Celtic mythology, there is a tale of a beautiful girl

from the OTHERWORLD who dwelt in the LAKE, Llyn-y-Fan Fach, near Llanddeusant. She was wooed by a local farmer's son and agreed to marry him, warning him that if he ever gave her three blows she would go back to the lake. After several years of marriage and farming, her husband forgot the warning and gave his wife three blows. She then went back to the lake, taking the livestock with her, but she left behind her three sons. According to one legend, the farmer tried to follow her and was drowned in the lake. Another legend has it that the dweller in the lake returned to see her sons when they grew up and gave them some medical recipes. Because of this the brothers became skilled physicians and were known as Meddygon Meddfai.

LOCH

In Irish Celtic mythology, Loch was the son of Mofebais. He was a champion warrior of Connacht who refused to fight CUCHULAINN because he did not wish to fight a youth without a beard. His opponent got round this problem by sticking some dried grass on his chin to simulate a beard. Loch wounded Cuchulainn but was eventually defeated and killed by him. As with many other legends, there are variations on the Loch legend.

LOCHLANN *see* LLYCHLYN.

LOCRINUS

In British mythology, Locrinus was a son of BRUTUS and brother of Albanactus and KAMBER. After his father died, he became the ruler of England and Albanactus became ruler of Scotland.

LODAN

In Irish Celtic mythology, Lodan was the son of LIR, the father of Sinend and the brother of MANANNAN MAC LIR.

LUCHTA *or* LUCHTAINE *or* LUCHTAR

In Irish Celtic mythology, Luchta was one of a triad of craft gods, Luchta being a wright or carpenter. With the other two, sometimes described as his brothers and called GOIBHNIU and Creidhne, he worked extremely quickly to make and repair the weapons of the TUATHA DE DANANN. The weapons were magical, in that anyone wounded by any of them would not recover.

LUGH

In Irish Celtic mythology, Lugh was one of the more important of the gods. He was associated with light and the SUN, and was also the god of arts and crafts. He is cognate with the British and Gaulish god LUGUS and the Welsh god LLUDD. LUGHNASADH is named after him. There are various accounts about his origins, and he is said to have become ruler of the gods after NUADA, king of the TUATHA DE DANANN, having demonstrated that he was capable of many skills and earning the name Samildanach, meaning 'of many skills'. As king of the Tuatha De Danann, he led them into the Second Battle of MAGH TUIREDH. In the battle he often took the form of someone with a single arm and a single eye. The FOMORII were defeated, and Lugh killed BALOR in single combat with a sling. There are various legends about Lugh.

LUGHNASADH

The Celts had four major festivals. One was Lughnasadh,

which was held on 1 August and was the Celtic harvest festival. It was so called because it was the feast of the god LUGH. Later it became the Christian festival of Lammas. The other three major festivals were SAMHAIN, IMBOLC and BELTANE.

LUGUS

In British and Gaulish Celtic mythology, Lugus was a god who gave his name to various place names in several lands, such as Lyons and Leiden. He is cognate with the Irish god LUGH and the Welsh LLUDD and is associated with the Roman god Mercury.

LUNED

In Welsh Celtic mythology, Luned was a girl who rescued OWAIN from prison and who gave him a ring to make him invisible. Later, Owain saved her life when she was about to be burnt alive.

LYONESSE

In British Celtic mythology, Lyonesse is said to have been a land off the south coast of Cornwall, famous for housing the remnants of the court of ARTHUR after the death of the king. The sea is said to have rushed over the land to prevent people following his knights.

M

MABINOGION

In Welsh Celtic mythology, Mabinogion is one of the most important source texts. It is based on two earlier manuscripts, *The White Book of Rhydderch* (1300–25) and *The Red Book of Hergest* (1375–1425). It consists of four tales concerning PWYLL, BRANWEN, MANAWYDAN FAB LLYR and MATH FAB MATHONWY. Later versions include the story of CULHWCH and OLWEN.

MABON

In Welsh Celtic mythology, Mabon was the son of MODRON. Legend has it that he was abducted from his mother when he was three days old and was incarcerated at Caer Loyw, which in the legend was synonymous with the OTHERWORLD. CULHWCH rescued him from captivity and in return he helped Culhwch find OLWEN and assisted him in fulfilling the tasks that needed to be accomplished before Culhwch could claim Olwen in marriage.

MAC CECHT

In Irish Celtic mythology, Mac Cecht was one of the TUATHA DE DANANN at the time of the invasion of Ireland by the Sons of MIL ESPAINE, who defeated the Tuatha. A son of OGHMA, he was the husband of the goddess Fotla or Fodla. He was killed by Eremon.

MAC CUILL
In Irish Celtic mythology, Mac Cuill was one of the Tuatha De Danann at the time of the invasion of Ireland by the Sons of Mil Espaine who defeated the Tuatha. He was the husband of the goddess Banbha or Banb and was killed by Eber.

MAC DA THO
In Irish Celtic mythology, Mac Da Tho was a king of Leinster who owned a huge pig and a hunting dog that was so fast it could run all around Leinster in a single day. To prevent his kingdom being attacked and taken from him, he promised his hound to both the likely attackers, representatives of Connacht and Ulster. The huge pig was slaughtered for a celebratory feast and an argument developed over which side got the larger portion. The people of Connacht and Ulster engaged in battle. There are various versions of this legend. In one the hound runs away. In another it is given the right to choose its new owner and chooses Ulster.

MAC GREINE
In Irish Celtic mythology, Mac Greine was one of the Tuatha De Danann rulers at the time of the invasion of Ireland by the Sons of Mil Espaine. The Tuatha were defeated by them. A son of Oghma, Mac Greine was the husband of the goddess Eriu, who gave her name to Eire or Ireland. He was killed by Amhairghin.

MACHA

In Irish Celtic mythology, Macha was a goddess who is sometimes taken to be one deity and sometimes taken to be three.
She was associated with war, fertility and the prosperity of
Ireland, and is also associated with horses. As a goddess associated with fertility, she was regarded as being a MOTHER-
GODDESS. As a war-goddess she did not actually take part in
battles but was present in the field and used her powers to
help one side or the other.

She is said to have been the wife of NEMEDH, the leader of
the third invasion of Ireland, and to have prophesied the
TAIN BO CUAILNGE, after which Macha died of a broken
heart. She is also said to have married NUADA and to have
been killed by BALOR. Another legend suggests that she
ruled Ireland as a warrior queen around 377 BC and established EMHAIN MACHA, the ancient capital of Ulster, to which
she gave her name. However, it has also been suggested that
the warrior queen was a different Macha whose exploits
have become confused with those of Macha.

Macha is also said to have been the wife of Crundchu or
Crunn-chu of Ulster. Her fame as a fast runner is said to
have led her husband to boast at the Ulster assembly that she
could outrun the king's horses. A race was arranged, and
Macha duly defeated the horses. However, she was heavily
pregnant at the time of the race and gave birth to twins and
died in childbirth, staying alive long enough to place a curse
on the men of Ulster. By this curse, from that time forth they
would feel the pains of childbirth when they were at critical
times in battle or any time of danger, thereby becoming ex-

tremely weak for five days and four nights. The only Ulster warrior to be exempt from the curse was CUCHULAINN.

MACSEN WLEDIG
The Roman emperor Maximus was known as Macsen Wledig in Welsh Celtic tradition. He is said to have married a Celt named ELEN. According to one tradition the emperor's standard, which showed a dragon on a purple background, was the origin of the Welsh red dragon banner.

MAEL DUIN *see* MAIL DUIN.

MAEVE *see* MEDB.

MAGA *see* ROSS THE RED.

MAGH TUIREDH *or* MOYTURA
In Irish Celtic mythology, Magh Tuiredh was the site of two famous battles. The first was fought between the TUATHA DE DANANN under NUADA against the FIR BHOLGS. Nuada's forces won, but he himself was badly wounded. According to one legend, he lost an arm and had it replaced by a silver one, but according to another, it was his head that he lost and had to have replaced.

The next battle was between Nuada's forces and the FOMORII. Nuada was slain according to one legend—according to another he abdicated. In either event, LUGH took over his leadership from him. The Tuatha De Danann had magical weapons forged by TRI DE DANA and had the help of Lugh's powers of sorcery. Lugh and BALOR eventually settled the battle by engaging in single combat. Lugh with his sling aimed at Balor's single eye, which could kill a whole army at a glance, and smashed Balor's eye and brains.

MAIDEN CASTLE *see* HILL FORT.

MAIL DUIN *or* MAEL DUIN

In Irish Celtic mythology, Mail Duin was the central character of one of the IMMRAM or invasion tales. He was the son of a nun who, according to legend, was raped by his father, AILILL, who was said to have come from Aran. Mail Duin with some companions set out on a voyage to find a group of raiders from overseas who murdered his father. The immram tells of their adventures on the voyage. They located the murderers but were advised by a hermit to spare their lives because God had protected them on their voyage. They did so and were guided home again by a falcon.

MAIL *or* MAEL FOTHARTAIG *or* FHOTHARTAIG

In Irish Celtic mythology, Mail Fothartaig was the son of RONAN and a very handsome man. His stepmother fell in love with him and made advances towards him, which he rejected. She accused him of rape. Reluctantly Ronan believed her and had him killed.

MANANNAN MAC LIR

In Irish Celtic mythology, Manannan mac Lir was the son of LIR. Like his father, he was a sea-god and is associated with sea journeys to the OTHERWORLD. Traditionally he is supposed to have lived on the ISLE OF MAN, of which he was the first king, although he is also supposed to have lived in Tir Tairnigirib, the Otherworldly Land of Promise. He is associ-

ated with the Welsh deity MANAWYDAN FAB LLYR. His wife
was FAND. He is usually shown as wearing a green cloak,
perhaps one that seemed to change colour when it caught the
light. He had the ability of SHAPE-CHANGING and is supposed to
have used this skill to father mortal children, such as MONGAN.
The sea was very important to Ireland, and Manannan mac
Lir was an important god, being able, for example, to create
storms to wreck invading ships. He was also associated with
trickery and sorcery, and is supposed to have given LUGH
magical gifts to help NUADA and him fight the FOMORII.

MANAWYDAN FAB LYR
In Welsh Celtic mythology, Manawydan fab Lyr was the son
of LLYR. He may be the Welsh equivalent of MANANNAN MAC
LIR, although there is not an exact parallel and there is no
evidence that he was considered to be a god of the sea. He is
said to have been the brother of BENDIGEID VRAN and BRANWEN,
and possibly a cousin of PRYDERI. He is also said to have been
the husband of RHIANNON. Manawydan and Pryderi with their
wives, CIGFA being Pryderi's wife, are said to have been at
their palace at Arbeth in Dyfed when a peal of thunder was
heard and a mist fell. When the mist cleared, the land was
barren, with no crops, cattle or people apart from the four in
the palace. One legend has it that after some time roaming in
the forests living off what they could find in the way of food,
the four went to England. After a series of adventures they
returned to Dyfed.
 Pryderi ignored Manawydan's warning and followed a
large white boar into a fort or castle. He saw a golden bowl

and laid his hands on it. He could not then let go of the bowl and was struck dumb. Rhiannon, who had followed him, suffered a similar fate, and they both disappeared into a mist.

There are variations on the legend of the adventures of the four. According to one, when Pryderi and Rhiannon disappeared, Manawydan promised to take care of Cigfa and set himself up as a cobbler, until he had earned enough money to establish a farm. However, he had ill luck with his grain crops. Twice he discovered that his entire crop had been eaten, and when the corn was ripe in the third year he kept watch so as to find out the reason for the destruction of the crops. On seeing a large quantity of mice, he caught one and took it home, threatening to hang the creature, despite Cigfa's efforts to point out the ridiculous nature of such a punishment. When he was preparing the miniature gallows for the execution, various members of the church passed—a poor cleric, a finely dressed priest and a bishop accompanied by his retinue. All of them offered Manawydan money to save the life of the mouse, but he was impervious to their offers until the bishop stopped offering money and told Manawydan that he could have whatever he wished in return for saving the life of the mouse. Not surprisingly, he elected to ask for the safe return of Pryderi and Rhiannon. The supposed bishop revealed that he was LLWYD and the mouse was in fact his wife. It had been Llwyd who had put a spell on Pryderi and Rhiannon because of what PWYLL, Pryderi's father, had done to Llwyd's friend GWAWL in depriving him of having Rhiannon as a wife.

MAON *see* LABHRAIDH LOINGSECH.

MARCAN *see* CANO.

MATH FAB MATHONWY

In Welsh Celtic mythology, Math fab Mathonwy was, as his name indicates, the son of MATHONWY. He was supposed to have to keep his level of vitality charged by constantly placing his feet in a virgin's lap, the virgin being known as a foot-holder, unless he was required to take part in a war. He had great powers of magic and was able to make people change shape. He may also have been associated with fertility.

GWYDION FAB DON manufactured a war between PRYDERI and Math to get Math out of the way so that Gwydion and his brother, GILFAETHWY, could rape Math's foot-holder, GOEWIN. Math punished the two by decreeing that they should spend the next three years as male and female animals—one year as deer, one year as swine, and the third year as wolves—each year producing at least one offspring. After the three years they were restored to their human shape, and Gwydion suggested his sister ARANRHOD as foot-holder, but she gave birth to twins while undergoing the virginity tests that applicants for the post of foot-holder had to undertake. One of the twins was LLEU LLAW GYFFES, and Gwydion helped the boy to overcome two curses put on him by his mother. Later Math and Gwydion made for Lleu BLODEUWEDD, a woman made of flowers, to obviate the third curse of Aranrhod.

MATHOLWCH

In Welsh Celtic mythology, Matholwch was a king of Ireland

who married BRANWEN in an attempt to promote good relations between Ireland and Wales, and who received a magic
CAULDRON from Branwen's brother, BENDIGEID VRAN or Bran
the Blessed. At the wedding feast he was insulted by EFNISIEN,
Branwen's half-brother, and in revenge mistreated Branwen

Hearing of this, Bendigeid and his followers sought vengeance for his sister's humiliation and invaded Ireland.
Matholwch's forces won at first because the magic cauldron
enabled wounded or dead Irish soldiers to be completely
healed or brought back to life if they were immersed in it.
Efnisien contrived to destroy the cauldron, and Matholwch's
forces were defeated. In the whole of Ireland the only people left were five pregnant women, who hid in a cave and
later gave birth to five boys whom they married, so that
eventually Ireland was repopulated. Only seven of the
Welsh expedition survived. Bendigeid suffered a mortal
blow and his head was taken by his followers to be buried in
Britain. Branwen returned to Wales to die of a broken heart
when she thought of the carnage that had occurred on her
behalf.

MEDB

In Irish Celtic mythology, Medb, whose name has several variants and is sometimes anglicized as Maeve, was a goddess-
queen of Connacht. Her name means 'she who intoxicates'
and is related to the word 'mead'. She is said to have been the
wife of nine Irish kings, and only someone who was her mate
could be a true king of Ireland. In all her various marriages
she was the dominant partner. Her promiscuity suggests fer-

tility and she also appears to have been regarded as a goddess of sovereignty.

Perhaps the most famous legend involving Medb is that in which she sets out to get possession of the great brown bull of Ulster, known as Donn Cuailnge. The young Ulster champion, Cuchulainn, fought valiantly but eventually he was killed by means of Medb's magic. The bull was taken by Medb, but it did battle with Finnbhenach, the bull belonging to Medb's husband, Ailill, which it destroyed. Legend has it that Medb was killed by her nephew, Furbaidhe, in revenge for the fact that Medb had murdered his mother. He is said to have killed her with a sling-shot and a lump of cheese.

MEDDYGON MEDDFAI *see* Llyn-y-Fan Fach.

MEICHE
In Irish Celtic mythology, Meiche was the son of Morrigan. He was killed by Dian Cecht because it was prophesied that he would bring disaster to Ireland. When he was dead, his body was cut open to reveal three hearts, one for each aspect of his mother, and according to one legend each of these hearts had a serpent growing in it. Two of the hearts were burnt but the third escaped and its huge serpent did indeed threaten disaster to Ireland but it too was killed by Dian Cecht.

MEDICINE
The Celts, particularly the Irish, were renowned for their medical skills, and during the Dark Ages the Irish medical schools were renowned throughout Europe. The oldest surviving medi-

cal manuscripts in Irish date from the early fourteenth century. In Irish Celtic mythology, DIAN CECHT was the god of medicine.

MERLIN
In Welsh Celtic mythology, Merlin was a wizard who played a major part in the Arthurian legends. The Welsh form of his name was MYRDDIN, and a character of this name played a part in Welsh mythology before ARTHUR and his knights came to the fore. GEOFFREY OF MONMOUTH describes Merlin and his exploits in *Libellus Merline* (Little Book of Merlin) which was written around AD 1135 and incorporated into his *Historia*.

MERMAIDS/MERMEN
As in several other cultures, especially those associated with the sea, mermaids and mermen, creatures that are half-human, half-fish, feature significantly in Celtic culture. Mermaids are represented as being beautiful and enticing creatures, although they are not always benevolent. Mermen are usually much uglier with small piggy eyes, red noses and green hair. Cornwall is particularly rich in mermaid lore. According to one legend a mermaid spirited away a squire's son from Zennor.

MESGEDRA *see* CONALL CERNACH.

MIDACH *see* DIAN CECHT.

MIDHIR
In Irish Celtic mythology, Midhir lived in the SIDH of Bri Leith, one of the underground kingdoms of the gods when they had

been driven from Ireland by the Sons of Mil Espaine. The most important story of Midhir concerns his courtship of Etain. He was married to Fuamnach but fell in love with Etain, and Oenghus helped him to bring her home as his new bride. Fuamnach was furious and took her revenge. There are variations on the legend. In one, Fuamnach turned Etain into a pool of water that turned into a worm that in turn became a huge and beautiful fly. Fuamnach then conjured up a huge gust of wind that blew the beautiful fly away until it fell on some rocks by the sea. After seven years she was discovered by Oenghus. He arranged for her to be returned to Midhir, but Fuamnach created another huge gust of wind that blew the fly into a glass of wine. The wine and the fly were swallowed by a pregnant woman and Etain was reborn. In time, she was married to the high king of Ireland Eochaidh Airemh. After that the legend becomes convoluted and the variations even more complex. Midhir tried to get his wife back and challenged the high king to a game of chess. Having won, he chose as his prize a kiss from Etain, but Eochaidh reneged on his bargain and would not let Midhir near Etain and would not let him into Tara. Midhir succeeded in gaining entrance, turned himself and Etain into swans and flew away up the central smoke hole of the room. Eochaidh pursued them, demanding the return of his wife. After various developments, Midhir produced fifty identical women, all looking like Etain. Eochaidh thought that he would choose among them carefully, but he accidentally chose his own daughter. It was only after she had borne him a son, the hero Conaire Mor, that he realized that he had committed incest.

MIL

In Irish Celtic mythology, Mil was the son or grandson of Bregon and the ancestor of the first human rulers of Ireland, who were known as the Sons of MIL ESPAINE. He was the brother or nephew of ITH, who led an invasion expedition from Spain to Ireland but was killed by the TUATHA DE DANANN. After Ith's body was returned to Spain, Mil organized another invading trip to Ireland. He did not reach it but his sons did, and they attempted to carry out the conquest of Ireland.

MILCHRU *see* PATRICK.

MIL ESPAINE, SONS OF *or* MILESIANS

In Irish Celtic mythology, the Sons of Mil Espaine were the sons and descendants of MIL. They landed in Ireland on the feast of BELTANE under the leadership of AMHAIRGHIN. The invaders defeated the TUATHA DE DANANN and set out for TARA. On their way they met three goddesses, Banbha, Fotla and ERIU, the wives of MAC CUILL, MAC CECHT and MAC GREINE. The invaders promised each goddess in turn that the land would always be called after her if she were to help them in their invasion quest. The help and advice of Eriu led the invaders to name the land Eire. The invaders defeated their opponents at the Battle of Tailtinn.

The Tuatha De Danann, having been defeated, deprived the invaders of milk and corn in an attempt to retrieve their land. In the end, the two sides decided to divide the land between them, the Tuatha De Danann getting the underground part. The part above ground went to the Sons of Mil Espaine, EREMON, a son of Mil, ruling the northern half of the country and EBER FINN, one of the leaders of the Sons of Mil Espaine, ruling the southern part. Later north and south went to war, Eber Finn was killed and Eremon became ruler of the whole kingdom, becoming the first human king to rule the whole of Ireland.

MIODCHAOIN

In Irish Celtic mythology, Miodchaoin was a warrior and friend of CIAN, who lived on a hill. He was placed under a bond never to permit anyone to shout from the summit of the hill. Miodchaoin had a fight with the three sons of TUIRENN when they arrived at the hill to complete the last of the tasks imposed on them by LUGH as their punishment for murdering Cian. Miodchaoin was killed and the three sons were barely alive after the fight. As they were dying, they succeeded in giving three weak shouts from the hill, thereby fulfilling the last of their punishment tasks. They then begged Lugh to heal them of their fatal wounds but he refused and all three died.

MINERVA *see* SULIS.

MISTLETOE

The Celts, particularly DRUIDS, were much connected with the partially parasitic plant mistletoe. It seems to have been regarded as a cure for barrenness if it was mixed in a drink, and it is likely to have been used in fertility rites. The OAK tree on which mistletoe grows was sacred to the druids. They used oak trees to form sacred groves and they used oak branches in sacred rites. When LINDOW MAN was discovered, he was found to have mistletoe pollen in his stomach, causing specu-

lation that he had taken part in some form of druidic human
SACRIFICE.

MODRON
In Welsh Celtic mythology, Modron, whose name means
'mother', was the mother of MABON. Her name is thought to
be a form of the Gaulish Matrona, and she is considered to
have been one of the MOTHER-GODDESSES.

MODEL WEAPONS
A tradition that the Celts shared with other early peoples was
that of making small replicas of weapons, such as swords,
spears and shields, and tools, such as axes and wheels. They
were used as votive offerings to the gods and as grave goods
to accompany dead people on their way to the OTHERWORLD.
Some appear to have been worn as talismans by the living.
Often great trouble was taken to make the model as close to
the original as possible.

MOEN *see* LABHRAIDH LOINGSECH.

MOFEBAIS *see* LOCH.

MOLMOTIUS *see* PINNER.

MONGAN
In Irish Celtic mythology, Mongan was supposedly the son of
Fiachna Lurgan, but in fact he was the son of the sea-god
MANANNAN MAC LIR who appeared before Fiachna's queen
when her husband was away in Scotland fighting. He told her
that unless she bore him a son her husband would die the next
day. She agreed, and the sea-god appeared the next day and

helped Fiachna win a great victory. When the boy was born, Manannan mac Lir took him away to live with him until he was about twelve.

Mongan married Dubh Lacha, who was abducted by Brandubh, king of Leinster. To retrieve his wife, Mongan used his sorcery skills inherited from his father and took the shape of Aed, son of the king of Connacht. He made an ugly old woman take the shape of IBHELL and asked Brandubh if he would like to exchange wives. He agreed, and the supposed Ibhell turned back into a hag.

Mongan is also said to be a reincarnation of FIONN MAC CUMHAILL, and parallels have been drawn between the legend of Mongan and the Arthurian legend.

Historically, there was a King Mongan who ruled at Moylinny on Lough Neagh and died around AD 625.

MORANN

In Irish Celtic mythology, Morann was a DRUID at the court of CONCHOBAR MAC NESSA. His father had ordered him to be drowned, but he was rescued and raised by a SMITH. He prophesied the arrival of CUCHULAINN and some of his famous deeds.

MORDA *see* CERRIDWEN.

MORFESSA

In Irish Celtic mythology, Morfessa was one of the wizards who taught the TUATHA DE DANANN their magic skills before they went to Ireland. He came from the city of FALIAS.

MORGEN

In Welsh Celtic mythology, Morgen was a druidic goddess

who had nine sisters and may have associations with MODRON. Various claims have been made for her, such as that she could fly on artificial wings, that she could change her shape and that she had great powers of healing, but there is a good deal of confusion surrounding her. She is thought to have been the original of the Morgan Le Fay of the Arthurian legend.

MORIATH *see* LABHRAIDH LOINGSECH.

MORRIGAN

In Irish Celtic mythology, Morrigan was one of a group of Irish war-goddesses who can be thought of as a single goddess or as a triple goddess. The war-goddesses did not actually take part in battles but they were present in the field and used their powers to help one side or the other. Morrigan was also associated with sexuality and fertility, this last association making her a MOTHER-GODDESS. In addition, she is said to have had powers of prophesy and the ability to cast spells. In her capacity of war-goddess, she helped the TUATHA DE DANANN at the Battles of MAGH TUIREDH, and her association with sexuality is demonstrated by the legend that she stood astride the River Unius with a foot on each bank and had sexual intercourse with the DAGHDA before the second battle. Her sexuality is also emphasized in the legend of how she made overtures to CUCHULAINN but was rejected by him, thereby ensuring that she bore him a terrible grudge.

Morrigan is also known for her ability in SHAPE-CHANGING. She frequently took the shape of a crow or a RAVEN.

MOTHER-GODDESS

The concept of abundance and fertility was important in Celtic culture. Various goddesses were associated with this concept, being regarded as divine earth-mothers, often being referred to as *matronae* in Gaul and the Rhineland. Such goddesses can often function both as single goddesses and as triple goddesses.

Mother-goddesses are often depicted on sculptures as wearing long garments and sometimes have one breast bared. They are often accompanied by some kind of symbol of fertility, such as babies, fruit or loaves, and are often presented in groups, although single images of mother-goddesses are also common.

In Irish Celtic mythology, the mother-goddess is prominent. They are often triple goddesses, being associated with other concepts as well as fertility. MACHA and MORRIGAN are cases in point.

MOUNTAINS

As is the case with LAKES, mountains were important in Celtic worship. For example, in the mountainous regions of GAUL a number of gods associated with high places were venerated. The Celtic god of the sky was also associated with mountains since they rose from the earth high into the boundaries of his kingdom.

MOYTURA *see* MAGH TUIREDH.

MURIAS

In Irish Celtic mythology, Murias was one of the four great

cities of the TUATHA DE DANANN. It was the home of SIMIAS, one of the wizards who helped to teach the Tuatha De Danann their magic skills before their arrival in Ireland. The magic CAULDRON of the DAGHDA is said to have come from Murias.

MUIREDACH, CROSS OF
One of the finest of the Irish HIGH CROSSES is the Cross of Muiredach, situated in the early Celtic settlement of Monaster-boice near Drogheda. The main sculpture on the circular head on the west side is an elaborate Crucifixion scene and on the east side is an elaborate Last Judgement scene. Some of the other carving is open to interpretation, some regarding it as depicting various events in Christ's life and others regarding it as depicting events relating to the Vikings, which had taken place around the ninth century just before the cross was erected.

MUIRNE *see* FIONN MAC CUMHAILL.

MYRDDIN
In Welsh Celtic mythology, Myrddin was the original Welsh name of MERLIN, who was the wizard in the Arthurian legends. There are many legends about him, some of them conflicting. He is supposed to have been the offspring of a nun and an evil spirit, thereby making him a fatherless child. Other traditions ascribe various fathers to him. He is said to have connections with VORTIGERN. One legend has it that the Vortigern was attempting to have a tower built on Dinas Emrys but it kept falling down. A solution of his advisers was to sacrifice a fatherless son, and Myrddin was chosen. When he

was taken to the site on which the tower was to be built, Myrddin advised the king that there were two dragons in a lake under the proposed site. An underground lake was uncovered and a red and white dragon appeared, an event that caused Myrddin to utter a series of prophecies.

Another legend has it that when Ambrosius Aurelius defeated Vortigern, he wished to erect a monument to mark the event and to commemorate the dead. Myrddin advised him to go to Ireland and bring back some of the stones that formed the GIANTS' RING. These were then erected as STONEHENGE on Salisbury Plain.

There are several other legends featuring the wizard, and many different versions as to how he met his death. Also there are many prophecies that have been ascribed to Myrddin, one forecasting a terrible end for Carmarthen.

One Welsh tradition suggests that Myrddin was not one person but three incarnations of the same person. The situation is made more confusing by the fact that historically there appears to have been not only one Myrddin but two. One was Myrddin Wyllt, who lived in Scotland, and one was Myrddin Emrys, who lived in Wales. It is the latter who became the Arthurian Merlin.

N

NAGES

At Nages near Nimes in Provence there was a Celtic shrine of which a lintel survives. It is particularly interesting because it has a carved stone frieze on which are depicted a number of severed HEADS alternating with galloping HORSES. It calls to mind the practice of Celts of collecting the scalps of their defeated enemies and attaching them to their horses when riding away from battles.

NAKED WARRIORS

In the Celtic world it was a custom of warriors to strip naked before rushing into battle, for example, against the Romans, or to engage in single combat. It has been suggested that this made them at one with nature and so increased their life force.

NANTOSVELTA

In Gaulish Celtic mythology, Nantosvelta was a goddess often associated with SUCELLUS as part of the divine couples. Her name, generally being taken to mean 'winding river', suggests that she is a WATER goddess but she is sometimes depicted as carrying the model of a house on a pole, suggesting that she is also associated with hearth and home. She is sometimes shown carrying a pot, which has been taken, like the CAULDRON, as a symbol of regeneration. Associated with prosperity and abundance, she also has connections with death, as is suggested by the presence of a RAVEN in several of her representations.

NAOISE

In Irish Celtic mythology, Naoise was the one of the three sons of Uisnech. He attracted the attention and love of DEIRDRE, who had been told by friends that he had the physical attributes that she sought—black hair, white skin and red cheeks. Naoise was at first reluctant to become involved since he knew that Deirdre had been betrothed since birth to CONCHOBAR MAC NESSA and also, more importantly, that CATHBAD had prophesied that Deirdre would be the most beautiful woman in the whole of Ireland but would cause terrible suffering and ruin. However, he fell in love with her, and when she challenged his honour he agreed to elope with her. In company with the brothers of Naoise, they went to Scotland. Conchobar sent a message to Naoise and his brothers that he had forgiven them and that they should return to Ireland. Deirdre dreamed that this was an act of treachery but the brothers refused to listen to her. She turned out to be right, because, when they arrived at EMHAIN MACHA, they were killed by Eoghan mac Durthacht with the sword given him by MANANNAN MAC LIR.

NATCHRANTAL

In Irish Celtic mythology, Natchrantal was a Connacht champion in MEDB's army. He fought with CUCHULAINN and gave Medb the excuse to push far into Ulster in order to take the DONN CUAILGNE, the great brown bull of Ulster, which Medb had long coveted.

NECHTAN *see* BOANN.

NECHTA SCENE

In Irish Celtic mythology, Nechta Scene was a monstrous being whose three sons, Foill, Fannell and Tuachell, were killed by CUCHULAINN.

NEIT *see* NET.

NEMAIN *or* **NEMHAIN**

In Irish Celtic mythology, Nemain was a war-goddess like MACHA and MORRIGAN. Although the war-goddesses did not themselves take part in battles, they often showed their influence, for example by striking terror into one of the armies. Nemain's name means 'frenzy', and she was famous for causing panic among warriors. In the war between Connacht and Ulster, she stirred up such terror in the men of Connacht that a hundred of them are said to have died of fright. She was the wife of NET.

NEMEDH *or* **NEMED**

In Irish Celtic mythology, Nemedh was the leader of the third invasion of Ireland. The previous inhabitants who had come to Ireland with PARTHOLAN had been destroyed by a plague. When Nemedh died, his people were defeated and subjugated by the FOMORII. They rebelled, and the Fomorii king was killed but only thirty of Nemedh's followers survived and they left Ireland looking for somewhere to settle.

NEMEDIANS

In Irish Celtic mythology Nemedians were followers of NEMEDH.

NEMETON
In Celtic times, a nemeton was a sacred grove, the Celts having a special veneration for woodlands.

NEMETONA
In Roman-Celtic mythology, Nemetona was a goddess associated with groves, her name being formed from NEMETON. An association between her and NEMAIN has been suggested.

NEMHAIN *see* NEMAIN.

NERA
In Irish Celtic mythology, Nera was an attendant of AILILL. He went on an adventure to the OTHERWORLD, where he married and had a son. His Otherworld wife warned him that she had foreseen their SIDH host attacking Ailill and his court on the feast of SAMHAIN. Nera left the Otherworld to warn them. Ailill sent out a company to destroy the sidh but Nera had already gone back to the Otherworld to his wife and could not return.

NESSA
In Irish Celtic mythology, Nessa was the mother of CONCHOBAR MAC NESSA, either by her husband, FACHTA, or by the druid CATHBAD. She was the lover of FERGUS MAC ROTH.

NET *or* NEIT
In Irish Celtic mythology, Net was a war-god. He was the husband of NEMAIN.

NIALL NOIGIALLACH
In Irish Celtic mythology, Niall Noigiallach was called 'Niall

of the Nine Hostages'. He is considered by some to have been a historical figure as well as having featured in legend. He was the founder of the fifth Irish province and established his capital at TARA. His descendants were the Ui Neill, and they gained control over the central and northern parts of Ireland. In legend they have sometimes become synonymous with the Sons of MIL ESPAINE.

NIAMH
In Irish Celtic mythology, there are three characters called Niamh. One was the daughter of MANANNAN MAC LIR and she became the lover of OISIN. Another married CONALL CERNACH but became the lover of CUCHULAINN. She begged him not to attack the sons of CALATIN for she knew that this would lead to his death. The third was the daughter of Celtchar, who married Conganchas mac Daire, a warrior whom no one could slay. She learned the secret of his invulnerability and revealed it to her father, who killed the warrior. She then married a son of CONCHOBAR MAC NESSA. According to some legends, the second and third Niamhs are the same and the details have become confused.

NISIEN
In Welsh Celtic mythology, Nisien was the brother of EFNISIEN and half-brother of BRAN, BRANWEN and the other children of LLYR. He was a peacemaker and mediator.

NUADA AIREGETLAMH
In Irish Celtic mythology, Nuada was a leader of the TUATHA DE DANANN. He lost an arm in the first battle of MAGH TUIREDH,

even although he owned a sword from which no one could escape. Because no one who was physically imperfect could be king of the Tuatha, he had to abdicate in favour of BRES. Later, the giant leech, DIAN CECHT, fitted him with an artificial silver arm and he became known as 'Nuada of the Silver Hand'. Bres was forced to abdicate and Nuada was reinstated. During the subsequent war, Nuada, who was afraid of BALOR, gave up his kingdom to LUGH who killed Balor in single combat.

NUMBERS

In Celtic mythology, numbers played a significant part. The odd numbers were particularly important, notably three, five, seven, nine and seventeen. Of the even numbers, twelve was important.

O

OAK

In Celtic culture, the oak tree had sacred connections, being associated with the DRUIDS. Indeed, it has been suggested that the word 'druid' might be derived from the root *dru*, meaning oak. The druids used oak TREES to form sacred groves and used oak branches in some of their rites. MISTLETOE, also used in druidic ritual, grows on oak trees. The oak was revered for its strength and its longevity, and was sometimes thought of as being representatives of the Tree of Life, which linked the mortal world with the OTHERWORLD. Oak trees were associated with the SKY, and solar gods and many of the Celtic images and carvings that have been uncovered in archaeological excavations have been found to be made of wood from oak trees, showing the regard in which these were held. Many of the Celtic sailing ships were made of oak, making these particularly durable. Oak was also used to build bridges and plank-built houses. In the Celtic Christian era, churches and monasteries in Ireland were often constructed near oak trees.

OCHAIN

In Irish Celtic mythology, Ochain was the magic shield belonging to CONCHOBAR MAC NESSA. When its owner was in danger, it gave out a moaning sound.

OENGHUS *or* AENGHUS

In Irish Celtic mythology, Oenghus was a god of love. He was a son of the DAGHDA, his mother being BOANN. Because his mother conceived him in the course of an illicit affair, her pregnancy was concealed by the sun standing still for nine months. Oenghus was thus supposedly conceived and born on the same day. There are several legends associated with Oenghus. In one, he dreams of a young woman whom he does not recognize and with whom he falls in love. He discovers she is CAER, daughter of ETHAL ANUBAL. She changes shape every other year and becomes a swan. The only time that Oenghus can get together with Caer is when she has the shape of a swan, and so he changes himself into a swan and flies off with her. In another legend, Oenghus helps MIDHIR marry ETAIN, only to have the first wife of Midhir, FUAMNACH, exact various forms of revenge on his new bride. In yet another legend, Oenghus helps DIARMAID, whom Oenghus had fostered, and GRAINNE against FIONN MAC CUMHAILL.

OGHAM

The earliest form of Irish writing, Ogham is frequently referred to in Irish Celtic mythology. Legend has it that it was the invention of OGHMA. In fact, it is thought to have been developed in the third and fourth centuries AD, although there have been claims that it was in use as early as the first century BC. The majority of existing examples of Ogham are to be found on stones, some in Scotland, some in Wales, but most in Ireland. About a third of all the stones showing Ogham are to be found in County Kerry. The script takes the form of a series of lines or notches and may be related to some, now lost, system of druidic writing. A book written in the fourteenth century entitled *Book of Ballymote* discusses Ogham and its characters and contains legends about the origins and uses of Ogham. The Ogham script is sometimes known as the Tree Alphabet because each letter takes the name of a tree.

OGHMA *or* OGMA

In Irish Celtic mythology, Oghma was the god of eloquence and literature. He was given the titles of Grianainech, referring to the fact that he had a sunny countenance, and Cermait, referring to the fact that he had a honeyed mouth. In legend, the invention of OGHAM, the early Irish script, is ascribed to him.

He was one of the TUATHA DE DANANN, and under the rule of BRES he was humiliated by being made to collect firewood. Oghma captured Orna, the magic sword of Tethra. He is depicted as a warrior and a poet, and sometimes as a guide of the dead to the OTHERWORLD. He is the Irish equivalent of the Gaulish god OGMIOS.

OGMIOS

In Gaulish Celtic mythology, Ogmios was the equivalent of the Irish Celtic god OGHMA. He was often depicted as an old man carrying a club and bow. Because of the latter fact and because he was also depicted sometimes as being very muscular, he has been associated with the classical hero Hercules. He was the god of eloquence and poetry and was described by the Greek writer Lucian of Samosata as being depicted being followed by a happy group of people whose ears were attached to his tongue by thin chains. Like Oghma, he is sometimes associated with guiding the dead to the OTHERWORLD.

OISIN *or* OSSIAN

In Irish Celtic mythology, Oisin was the son of FIONN MAC CUM-HAILL and SADB and the father of OSCAR. His mother was changed into a deer by a druid, and when he was found by his father he called him Oisin, meaning 'fawn'. He is said to have grown up to be a great warrior and a great poet. According to legend, NIAMH fell in love with him and took him to live in the OTHERWORLD. When he thought that he had been with her long enough, he decided to return to his home, but in fact he had been away for three centuries. He was warned by Niamh not to dismount from the white horse that she gave him for his journey, but he ignored this warning when he stopped to help some peasants who were trying to move a very heavy stone. At his dismounting he became a very old man on the verge of death instead of the young man that the magic of Niamh and the Otherworld had preserved him as. He is said to have been taken to St PATRICK, whose scribes recorded what he said before he died.

OLLAV FOLA

The only king of Ireland said to have reached the highest rank of the druids, Ollav Fola is thought to have reigned around 1000 BC. The eighteenth ruler of Ireland, he is credited with giving the country a legal system and with setting up the triennial fair at TARA, where bards, musicians, etc, gathered to

175

record the history of the country and where legal disputes were settled.

OLWEN

In Welsh Celtic mythology, Olwen, whose name translates as 'white track', perhaps because four white trefoils are said to have sprung up wherever she walked, was the daughter of the chief giant, YSPADDADEN. CULHWCH had been advised that she was the only woman for him, and he set out to find her, a task that proved arduous. He eventually found her and then had to carry out a series of virtually impossible tasks set by the giant. These Culhwch succeeded in performing, but the giant continued to stipulate further conditions, and Culhwch eventually attacked the giant's fortress with the help of some of the many people who were the giant's enemies. Yspaddaden was killed and Olwen married Culhwch.

ORAL TRADITION

The Celtic tradition was essentially an oral one, and it was not until early Christian times that the Celts were to be found recording things in writing in their own language, whether this was legend, history, poetry or law. This inclination towards an oral tradition was not because of lack of education on the part of the Celts but seems to have been a matter of choice. That the Celts were capable of writing things down is shown by the various inscriptions associated, for example, with gravestones, of the kind, written in the characters of Latin and Greek, that have been found in Italy and Spain and linked to the Celtic culture.

Julius Caesar commented on the phenomenal amount of

material memorized by the Celts and on the fact that the Celts seemed to think that it was improper to commit things to writing. This dislike of the written word may have been associated with their religion. Certainly the Celts seem to have been associated with secrecy and mystery. It has been suggested that when the Greeks gave the name of KELTOI to the Celts they were simply putting on record a form of the name with which the Celts referred to themselves and which meant 'secret people'.

The oral tradition is obviously a source of frustration to historians because it has added considerably to the mystique of the Celts and to the difficulty in establishing facts about them as a people. Most of the legend and history that was eventually recorded in writing had been handed down orally for a thousand years, obviously varying as the handing-down process went on.

ORAN
The brother of St Columba (*see* IONA) was known as Oran. He is said to have volunteered to die so that Columba could consecrate with a burial the ground on which he wished to build his chapel.

ORDOVICES
One of the tribes that supported CARATACUS against the Roman invaders was a northern Welsh tribe known as Ordovices.

ORNA *see* OGHMA.

OSCAR
In Irish Celtic mythology, Oscar was the son of OISIN. He was

a mighty warrior and distinguished himself by killing a huge boar that many others had failed to catch. Oscar killed three kings in his first battle but also accidentally killed his best friend, Linne. He was in charge of a powerful battalion called 'The Terrible Broom', so called because it swept its enemies before it. He was married to Aidin, who died of a broken heart when he was mortally wounded in the Battle of GABHRA.

OSSIAN *see* OISIN.

OTHERWORLD
In Celtic mythology, Otherworld was, among other things, a name for the place where people's souls went after death to be reborn, it being part of the Celtic doctrine to believe in the IMMORTALITY of the soul. On the night of the feast of SAMHAIN, the Otherworld was said to be visible to mankind and its gates were opened wide. Legend has it that the inhabitants of the Otherworld then wreaked vengeance on any inhabitants of the mortal world who had done them wrong during their lives. Mortal humans could travel to the Otherworld while they were still alive but, although they retained their youth while they were there, they aged to their actual age when they returned. This was the fate that befell OISIN when he went to live with NIAMH and then returned.

The Otherworld was also the land of the gods. The Irish Other-world of the gods consisted of a series of sidhe (*see* SIDH), each with its own inexhaustible CAULDRON designed for perpetual feasting. The sidhe were the dwelling-places of the TUATHA DE DANANN and were thought of as lying underneath the country of Ireland. The Tuatha were allotted this underground world by the Sons of MIL ESPAINE, the first mortals to rule Ireland.

In Welsh Celtic mythology the Otherworld was known as ANNW.

The Otherworld was often perceived as being located on an island or islands to the west of Wales or Ireland and was not only the land of the dead but the land of youth, the land of happiness or the land of the promise. However, some mortals, when visiting it when still alive, such as CUCHULAINN, experienced the dark side of it and encountered monsters and other horrors

OWAIN

Historically, Owain was the son of URIEN. Although he is thought to have lived after the traditional Arthurian period— he is said to have defeated the British heavily in AD 593—in Welsh Celtic mythology Owain has passed into Arthurian legend along with his father. In legend, he is said to have been the son of Urien and ARTHUR's sister, Morgan Le Fay. Legend has it that he defeated the Black Knight, found the Castle of the Fountain, was imprisoned in it and rescued by LUNED, a girl who gave him a ring to make him invisible and helped him marry the Lady of the Fountain. When, after three years, his companions from the court of Arthur came looking for him, he returned with them and forgot the Lady of the Fountain. She pursued him and castigate him for his treachery and deception, and he fled from the court to become a recluse in another country. When he was very close to death, he was restored to life and strength by a noblewoman using magical means. After he has slain a lion and a serpent, he finds Luned imprisoned and under threat of death by burning. Having rescued her and other maidens and defeated a giant, he returned to the Lady of the Fountain.

P

PARTHOLAN *or* **PARYTHOLON**
In Irish Celtic mythology, Partholan was said to have been the son of SERA and the leader of one of the invasions of Ireland. Some ascribe the second invasion to him and others the third. With his companions, the Parthalians, he is said to have defeated the FOMORII and forced them into exile in the Hebrides and the Isle of Man. He and his people are then said to have cleared four plains and created seven lakes, as well as introducing brewing of ale and crafts, establishing the first hostel and establishing laws. Partholan is thus credited with bringing civilization to Ireland.

According to one legend, Partholan murdered his father and mother. He is said to have been the been the father of RURY. He and his followers are said to have been wiped out by a plague, with only Tuan mac Stern surviving.

PATRICK, ST
The patron saint of Ireland is Patrick. There are various legends about him, and although he is a historical figure, the legends have tended to obscure the facts. He is said to have been born in South Wales, the son of a Christian deacon who was a Roman citizen and a man of considerable means. Patrick

181

is said to have been captured by a group of Scoti, Irish raiders, who attacked his father's country estates. He was taken to Ireland, where he was taken into slavery, his master perhaps being an Antrim chief called Milchru. Six years later, guided by a dream, he walked a long way until he reached a harbour. From there a merchant ship is said to have taken him across the sea to a country that was possibly France, where he may have studied to become a monk.

After some time he is said to have returned to Britain, where he became a deacon and a priest. He was made a bishop and went to Ireland as a missionary. In this capacity he travelled as far as Cashel in the south and Ulster in the north, concentrating his efforts on converting the chiefs. He established a bishop's see at Armagh, where he is said to be buried, having died at Saul in Ireland. However, another theory suggests that he died at GLASTONBURY, where he had become abbot.

One of the legends involving St Patrick concerns the conversion of King Aenghus at Cashel. The saint is said to have accidentally pierced the king's foot with his bishop's crozier in the course of the formal religious ceremony. The king did not cry out, possibly because he thought it was part of the ceremony.

Another legend relating to St Patrick also took place in Cashel. Satan, supposedly being pursued by Patrick, encountered a mountain in his way and took a great bite out of it in order to pass through. The mountain became known as the Devil's Bite. Satan became tired of being weighed down by his heavy lump of rock as he fled and dropped it at Cashel, creating the rock there.

Some literary works of St Patrick remain extant—
Confessio, a kind of autobiography written in rather crude
Latin, and a letter addressed to a British chieftain who had
carried off as slaves some Irish Christians. His writings
give almost no exact dates and almost no geographical
detail. There is some disagreement about his date of
birth. Some ascribe to the theory that he was born around
AD 389, became a slave in 405, returned to Ireland in 432
and died in 461. Others think he was captured in the 430s,
returned to Ireland between 450 and 460, and died soon after
491.

PEBIN *see* GOEWIN.

PENARDUN
In Welsh Celtic mythology, Penardun is said to have been the
daughter of DON and the wife of LLYR. One legend has it that
she was the mother of MANAWYDAN FAB LYR, BRANWEN and
BENDIGEID VRAN. Another has it that she was not the mother
of Bendigeid and Branwen, ascribing their birth to Iweriadd.
Penardun is said to have later borne NISIEN and EFNISIEN to
Eurosswydd.

PENDARAN DYFED
In Welsh Celtic mythology, Pendaran Dyfed is a swineherd
who is the foster father of PRYDERI.

PEREDUR
In Welsh Celtic mythology, Peredur was the son of Efrawg.
He is the model of Percival of the Arthurian legends, who
went on quests to find the Holy GRAIL.

PHALLUS

In Celtic culture the phallus was a symbol of maleness and of fertility. The Celtic male deities were frequently depicted as having exaggeratedly large phalluses, indicating the Celts' preoccupation with fertility. In the northern parts of Britain, representations of naked gods of war were often shown with HORNS and with extremely large erect phalluses.

PICTS

This is the name given to the people who inhabited northern Britain in Roman times. Their name is first recorded around AD 297 in a Latin poem. The name means 'painted people' and was given to them by the Romans because they painted their bodies before going into battle in order to give them a fierce appearance. They appear to have been a confederation of several northern tribes.

There is some dispute as to whether the Picts, or at least all of them, were Celtic in origin, although it is acknowledged that their original name for themselves was Priteni, which is Celtic in origin, that some of the recorded tribal names are Celtic in origin and that some of them appear to have spoken a Celtic language. There is also dispute about where the Picts originally came from. Bede indicates that they came from Scythia, a region nowadays part of the Ukraine, but the medieval Irish poet Mael Mura of Othain indicates that they came from Thrace. There is also some dispute as to whether or not they preceded the ancient Britons.

PIGS

The Celts appear to have held pigs in high regard. There are frequent references to them in Celtic legend, often connected with some form of magic. For example, Easal, King of the Golden Pillars, gave to the sons of TUIREANN seven magic pigs that could be killed and eaten and yet be still alive next day. People who ate the flesh of any of these pigs were said to be immune to disease.

PILLAR CROSSES

The HIGH CROSSES that were very popular with the Celts had their origins in pillar crosses. The early pillar crosses were standing stones with designs carved on them, and they gradually evolved over several hundred years into the great intricate high crosses.

PILLARS

In Celtic culture, pillars played a large part. Sometimes they were made of wood and sometimes of stone. They were frequently erected at places that were regarded as being sacred. They may have been regarded by the Celts as representations of TREES, several of which were also held to be sacred. The pillars were often very tall and many of them depicted carvings of various kinds.

PINNER

In British Celtic mythology, Pinner was a king of England who was defeated and killed by Molmotius, who was set on expanding the kingdom of Cornwall, which he had inherited from his father.

PORREX

In British Celtic mythology, Porrex was a prince of Britain.

According to GEOFFREY OF MONMOUTH, he was a descendant of BRUTUS and was the son of GORBODUC and JUDON. Porrex had a brother, FERREX, with whom he quarrelled over the right of succession. Ferrex, nervous of his brother's hostile intentions, fled to GAUL and returned with an army. This, however, did not save him, as he was defeated and killed. Their mother, Judon, was so distraught at the loss of her younger son that she went mad and hacked Porrex to pieces as he lay sleeping. Thus both the potential heirs to the throne were dead, and, when Gorboduc himself died, the line descending from Brutus died out.

PRASUTAGUS

In British Celtic mythology, Prasutagus was the husband of BOUDICCA. He was the chief of the tribe ICENI, who were under Roman rule in Britain but had retained a degree of autonomy. After his death, the Romans took advantage of the situation and pillaged possessions that had belonged to Prasutagus and his family. They also are said to have had Boudicca flogged and to have raped her daughters. Their actions made Boudicca anxious for revenge, and she led a rebellion against the Romans. The rebellion was a spirited one and met with some initial success, but in the end it proved unsuccessful.

PRYDEIN

In British Celtic mythology, Prydein is said to have been a king of Cornwall who conquered the rest of Britain after PORREX's death. Some sources indicate that Britain may be named after him.

PRYDERI

In Welsh Celtic mythology, Pryderi was the son of PWYLL and RHIANNON, born after his parents had almost given up hope of Rhiannon conceiving. When Pryderi was just a few days old, he mysteriously disappeared. The women who were responsible for looking after the baby were terrified on discovering his disappearance and, to forestall charges of negligence, decided to blame Rhiannon. They told Pwyll that she had killed the baby and disposed of the body, making the charge more plausible by smearing her hands with blood as she slept. Fortunately for Rhiannon, Pwyll refused to believe that she had had anything to do with the baby's disappearance. However, Rhiannon was so distraught that she decided to do penance. Under the terms of the penance she carried those visitors to Pwyll's castle who wished to avail themselves of the offer.

All the while, Pryderi was quite safe. He was found by TEYRNON, lord of Gwent Is-Coed, who, with his wife, looked after the boy and brought him up. They named him Gwri, meaning 'golden hair'. Supposedly Teyrnon had been experiencing instances of the disappearance of the newborn before the arrival of Pryderi, but foals, not mortal infants, were involved. Every year, in May, his prized mare had given birth to a foal and every year the foal had disappeared shortly after its birth. On the night that he was to find Pryderi, Teyrnon kept watch over his pregnant mare and saw her give birth to a foal. At that point the foal was snatched by a huge claw that came through the window. He cut off the claw and saved the foal, and went outside to investigate a great noise. There he found the infant Pryderi.

This legend is probably connected with the fact that Rhiannon, mother of Pryderi, had connections with horses.

A few years into his boyhood, the actual number varying according to various forms of the legend, it was realized that Pryderi bore a striking resemblance to Pwyll, lord of Dyfed. The boy was reintroduced to his parents and renamed Pryderi by his mother in recognition of the worry and grief that his disappearance had occasioned.

Pryderi is said to have been a member of the expedition led by BENDIGEID VRAN to Ireland to retrieve BRANWEN. Many members of the expedition perished, but Pryderi was one of the seven survivors who journeyed for over eighty years before returning home after leaving Ireland. On the death of his father, Pryderi became lord of Dyfed, and Rhiannon, Pwyll's widow, married MANAWYDAN FAB LLYR. By that time Pryderi had married CIGFA.

Pryderi, Cigfa, Manawydan and Rhiannon had various adventures and for a while disappeared, thanks to a spell set on them by LLWYD, who was taking revenge for the treatment meted out to his friend GWAWL by Pwyll, Pryderi's father. Later, the two are released from the enchantment. For details of some of the legendary material surrounding their adventures, *see* MANAWYDAN.

For details of the story of Pryderi that relates to Gilfaethwy and Gwydion and for details of his death, *see* GILFAETHWY.

PWYLL

In Welsh Celtic mythology, Pwyll was a lord of Dyfed whose chief court was at Arbeth. Legend has it that he was out hunting one day when he saw a pack of strange hunting hounds pursuing and overcoming a stag. He chased away the hounds from the stag and set his own hounds on it instead. At that point a horseman appeared to complain about having his hounds called off. He regarded Pwyll's treatment as an insult and declared enmity on him. Discovering that the horseman was ARAWN, king of ANNW, an Otherworld country, Pwyll offered to make recompense for the insult, and Arawn replied that he could so by doing him a favour. The favour was that Pwyll should exchange physical forms with Arawn for a year, Pwyll in the shape of Arawn going to rule in Annw for a year and Arawn in the shape of Pwyll going to become lord of Dyfed for a year. At the end of his year in Arawn, Pwyll was to meet in combat and to try to kill HAFGAN, king of another Otherworld region and Arawn's declared enemy. Arawn warned Pwyll that he must be sure to kill Hafgan with one blow, for, if he dealt more than one blow, Hafgan would recover quickly and fight with even more vigour and spirit than before. Pwyll succeeded in killing Hafgan and he and Arawn then reverted to their original shapes and went back to their own countries, having become friends.

Another legend about Pwyll concerns RHIANNON. The story goes that when Pwyll first saw her he was captivated by her extreme beauty and immediately wished to marry her. Her father, HEFEYDD HEN, agreed to the couple being betrothed, the wedding to take place a year later. A variation on the theme is that Pwyll first saw Rhiannon out riding. She passed him and his men and, despite the fact that her horse did not seem to be going very fast, they did not seem to be able to catch up with her. Pwyll called out to her and she stopped. Then she confessed that she wanted to leave her suitor GWAWL and marry him instead.

Thus, a year after becoming betrothed to Rhiannon Pwyll made his way to Hefeydd's house for the wedding feast. At the feast Pwyll was approached by a handsome, smartly dressed young man who asked him for a favour. Pwyll, without identifying the nature of the favour, agreed to the request. Then he found out his mistake. The young man turned out to be Gwawl, who had been Rhiannon's suitor before she met Pwyll, and the unnamed favour that Pwyll had acceded to was the hand of Rhiannon in marriage. Pwyll had to honour the granting of the favour. Rhiannon, however, thought of a plan. She asked Gwawl to postpone the granting of the favour for a year, after which time she would marry him. When it came time for the wedding, she arranged for Pwyll and a number of his men to stand outside the hall where the wedding feast was taking place. Pwyll then entered the hall dressed as a ragged beggar and carrying a large sack. As arranged with Rhiannon beforehand, he asked for the sack to be filled with food from the feast. Rhiannon acceded to this request and asked Gwawl to push the food right down to the bottom of the sack. She then pushed him in and captured him in the sack, at which point Pwyll and his men rushed in and started kicking the sack until, Gwawl begged for mercy. Before they released him, they made him agree to give up any rights to Rhiannon's hand in marriage ever again and to promise not to seek revenge. Pwyll and Rhiannon were married and after a few years had a son, PRYDERI.

R

RAM
In Celtic culture, the ram was a common image. It was associated with the Romano-Celtic version of Mercury, as was the original classical god, Mercury. Small figures of rams belonging to the cult of Mercury have been found in parts of Britain and Gaul. The ram was associated in the Celtic world with war cults. Some of the Celtic war-gods in northern Britain were found depicted with ram HORNS, rams being associated with aggression and often sexual in nature. Some of the war-gods not only wore ram's horns but also were naked, suggesting virility and fertility as well as aggression and belligerence. Artefacts containing ram motifs have been uncovered by archaeologists at various Celtic sites, including LA TÈNE. For example, a flagon might have ram head motifs for handles.

RED BRANCH
In Irish Celtic mythology, the Red Branch was the collective name given to the group of heroic warriors at the court of CONCHOBAR MAC NESSA. There is some difference of opinion as to the origin of the name. Some think that it came from the fact that they had their regular gatherings in a red room in the

palace at EMHAIN MACHA. Other sources have it that ROSS THE
RED of Ulster gave his name to the group.

RAVEN

Traditionally ravens were associated with darkness but were
also associated with prognostication, and the raven is frequently credited with prognostic powers in Irish Celtic literature. For example, they are said to have warned LUGH of the
approach of the FOMORII. The raven was also associated with
battle, gloating over the bloodshed or foretelling the outcome
of the battle. BADB, a war-goddess, frequently took the shape
of a raven when she was present at a battle. The appearance
of Badb in raven guise was often taken as an prognostication
that someone was going to die.

RHEINHEIM

In 1954 the burial place of a Celtic princess was uncovered at
Rheinheim. She had been buried with a great deal of jewellery made of gold, bronze, amber and coral. As well as having been supplied with food and drink for her journey to the
next world, she had been supplied with a mirror. The grave
goods point to the belief of the Celts that the dead person was
simply moving from one world to another and would have
need of worldly goods. She is thought to have been buried in
the fourth century BC.

RHIANNON

In Welsh Celtic mythology, Rhiannon was the daughter of
HEFEYDD HEN and extremely beautiful. Her name means 'great
queen', and she became the wife of PWYLL. Legend has it that

Pwyll saw Rhiannon riding by on a fine white horse and fell instantly in love with her. He sought her hand in marriage and, although they eventually did marry, things did not go smoothly. For the story of the events leading to their wedding, *see* PWYLL. Rhiannon and Pwyll had a son after they had been married about four years. Once again, things did not go smoothly and the child was spirited away when he was a few days old. For the story of this and further details about the son, *see* PRYDERI. Rhiannon, after Pwyll's death, married Manawydan fab Llyr. For her adventures with him, *see* MANAWYDAN FAB LLYR. Rhiannon is associated in legend with horses and this has led to her being associated with EPONA, the Celtic horse goddess.

RIGDONN *see* RUADH.

RITUAL DAMAGE
As was the case with the peoples of the classical world, the Celts often deliberately broke or damaged things that were being offered as votive gifts to the gods. This was true of such things as pieces of pottery, but it was even more true of weapons. Thus, broken swords, etc, have been uncovered at former shrines to the gods and have been retrieved from burial chambers. It is as though whatever was offered as a gift to a god had to be rendered useless for earthly use before it was acceptable to a deity.

RIVERS
WATER generally was important to the Celts and rivers were often regarded as having their own spirit or river-god. It was

a common practice to throw valuable weapons, body armour, coins and jewellery into rivers as offerings to the river spirit or river-god.

ROC

In Irish Celtic mythology, Roc was the steward of Oenghus, the love god. The wife of Donn had a son by Roc, and Donn was so enraged that he killed the child by crushing it to death. Roc used his magical powers to restore life to the child, but it came back to life as Beann Ghulban, a monstrous boar without ears or tail. Roc placed the boar under a bond to kill Diarmaid, the son of Donn. Some time later, when Diarmaid was out hunting, he encountered the boar, which gored him and mortally wounded him.

RONAN

In Irish Celtic mythology, Ronan was a king of Leinster. He was the father of Mail Fhothartaig and the husband of Ethne. When she died, he married the daughter of Eochaidh, but she was young and had her heart set not on the father but on the son. She made advances to Mail, who rejected them, and, furious at being spurned, she told Ronan that Mail had attempted to rape her. Ronan at first refused to believe her accusations against his son, but she was persuasive and convinced him. He then ordered his son to be killed but is subsequently said to have learned the truth and to have died of grief. The lying wife then poisoned herself.

ROSMERTA

In Gaulish and British Celtic mythology, Rosmerta was a goddess associated with material wealth and prosperity. Indeed, her name means 'great provider'. She was the patron saint of merchants. She is associated with the Roman god Mercury, who became a Romano-Celtic god, and images of her accompanied by him were quite common, both carrying a purse and caduceus, which were associated with Mercury. It is quite possible that Rosmerta predated the Roman-Celtic Mercury. At any rate, images of her appeared unaccompanied by him. She was sometimes depicted as carrying a basket of fruit or cornucopia, symbols of plenty, and sometimes as carrying a churn or a bucket and ladle. The bucket, like the CAULDRON, may be a symbol of regeneration.

ROSS THE RED
In Irish Celtic mythology, Ross the Red was a king of Leinster. He is thought by some to have given his epithet to the RED BRANCH, although another reason given for this is that the group had their meetings in a red room. He married Maga, daughter of OENGHUS, and she bore him a son, a GIANT called FACHTNA. Fachtna married NESSA and became the father of CONCHOBAR MAC NESSA.

ROSUALT
In Irish Celtic mythology, Rosualt was a sea monster that was washed up on the Plain of Murrish in County Mayo. The monster is said to have vomited violently three times in three successive years before it died. Its vomiting had disastrous effects. The first bout destroyed all the fish and other sea creatures, the second destroyed all the birds of the air, and the third destroyed all the people and animals on the land.

ROUND HOUSES *see* HOUSES.

RUADAN

In Irish Celtic mythology, Ruadan was a son of BRES and the goddess BRIGID. He wounded the SMITH god GOIBHNIU at the second Battle of MAGH TUIREDH, but was mortally wounded in combat by the smith god with one of his magical weapons. His mother pleaded with Goibhniu to let her son be healed by DIAN CECHT and so live, but in vain. Brigid went to the battlefield to mourn for her son, and her lamentations are supposed to be the first 'keening' to be heard in Ireland.

RUADH

In Irish Celtic mythology, Ruadh, a son of Rigdonn, was on a sailing expedition, perhaps to Norway, when the ships suddenly became completely becalmed, even although the sails were still filled with wind. There is more than one version of this legend.

In one, Ruadh dived into the ocean and went under the ships to see if anything was impeding their progress. There he discovered three giantesses who were holding on to the ships and preventing them from moving. In order to have his ships able to continue with their voyage, Ruadh went with the giantesses to their home beneath the sea and became the lover of each of them. The giantesses told Ruadh that they would collectively bear him a son and asked him to visit them and see his son on his return voyage. Ruadh's ships then set off on the remainder of their voyage, but he completely forgot his promise to the giantesses and did not visit them. They took their revenge by cutting off the head of the son whom they had borne by him and threw it after Ruadh.

According to another version, when the ships became becalmed Ruadh and his crew ran out of food and water and he swam off in search of help. He came to an island under the sea where lived nine beautiful women. He spent nine nights with them and one of them bore him a son.

RUMHOL *see* LANHERNE CRUCIFIXION CROSS.

RURY
In Irish Celtic mythology, Rury was the son of PARTHOLAN. A LAKE is said to have sprung forth from Rury's grave and became known as Lake Rury.

S

SAAR *or* **SABIA** *see* SADB.

SACRIFICE, HUMAN
There is little definite archaeological evidence that the Celts
went in for human sacrifice. There are certainly examples of
what appear to be abnormal burials, but a distinction must be
made between people who died naturally and were then sub-
jected to some form of religious ritualistic activity and people who were ritually killed. There is much evidence of abnormal burial practices but whether this was or was not a fol-
low-on from natural death or sacrificial ritual murder is by no
means clear. For example, the infants who were buried as foun-
dation deposits at shrines, sometimes having been first decapitated, might have died naturally or they might have been
murdered.

LINDOW MAN, however, the young man who had been pole-
axed, garrotted and had his throat cut before being buried in
a bog, seems to point to ritual murder, but, of course, ritual
murder might have been administered as a punishment
rather than as a form of human sacrifice.

Although archaeological evidence does not seem to point
very clearly at the practice of human sacrifice among the

Celts, the writings of some Mediterranean commentators does draw attention to such a practice, particularly among the druids. Strabo, a Greek writer, described the druidic practice of stabbing victims and using their observations of their dying struggles to prophesy what was going to happen in the future.

SADB *or* SAAR *or* SABIA

In Irish Celtic mythology, Sadb was turned into a fawn by a DRUID. FIONN MAC CUMHAILL came across her when he was out hunting. Sadb took on her mortal form and became Fionn's mistress or wife. The druid discovered that she was no longer a fawn and turned her back into this form. Fionn then lost track of her, but one day he came across a naked boy who had been raised in the form of a fawn. He realized that the boy was his son by Sadb and called him OISIN, which meant 'little fawn'.

SALII *see* HEAD.

SALMON OF KNOWLEDGE

In Irish and Welsh Celtic mythology, the salmon was a symbol of wisdom and knowledge. One story involving salmon concerns FIONN MAC CUMHAILL. He went to see FINEGAS, the druid, who was to teach him poetry and knowledge. Finegas had been trying to catch a salmon, known as the salmon of knowledge, for several years. Sources differ as to whether Fionn or the druid actually eventually caught the fish but, either way, the fish was given to Fionn to cook. While he was cooking the fish, Fionn burnt his thumb on the fish and put it into his mouth to cool down and instantly received the gift of knowledge and wisdom. Finegas told him that it had been prophesied that Fionn would eat the fish and gave it to him, saying that he could no longer teach him anything that he did not know. The salmon is supposed to have acquired its gift of knowledge from having eaten the nuts of hazel trees that grew at the bottom of the sea.

SALT

In several Celtic sites in Europe the wealth of the inhabitants was based on salt. The famous site at HALLSTATT, the excavation of which greatly increased our knowledge of the Celts, was named after a salt-mining settlement in Upper Austria.

SAMHAIN

One of the four major Celtic festivals, Samhain was celebrated on 1 November and on the night that preceded it, making it in terms of time the equivalent of the modern HALLOWEEN. A pastoral festival, Samhain marked the passing of one pastoral year and the beginning of another year. At the time of Samhain, the livestock were brought in from the fields, some to be slaughtered for food and others to be kept for breeding purposes during the festival. Samhain was also the time when the usual barriers between the mortal world and the OTHERWORLD were suspended. At Sam
hain there were great gatherings at TARA, and people met to feast and take part in fairs, markets and horse races. It was thought that spirits from the Otherworld could freely visit the mortal world and that mortals could see and penetrate the Otherworld. This connection between Samhain and the su-

pernatural corresponds to the connection between witches and other supernatural forces and Halloween. Ritual fires were lit but only after all fires were extinguished and relit from a ceremonial fire lit by the DRUIDS.

Samhain was a time of great significance to the Celts, and their legends reflect the strange and important things that happened on the festival. For example, it was the time that the people of NEMEDH had to pay their annual tribute to the FOMORII, a tribute that was extremely crippling, consisting as it did of two-thirds of their corn, wine (some legends say milk) and children. It was also the date of the second battle of MAGH TUIREDH, and on the night before Samhain the DAGHDA mated with MORRIGAN as she straddled the River Unius. Samhain was the time of year when Aillen annually burned down Tara, after lulling the guards to sleep with enchanted music, until he was killed by FIONN MAC CUMHAILL.

SAMHAIR

In Irish Celtic mythology, Samhair was the daughter of FIONN MAC CUMHAILL. She was the wife of Cormac Cas, who is recorded as living in the third century AD. He is supposed to have built a great palace for his bride and a bed supported on three stone PILLARS. The palace was thus named Dun-tri-lag, the 'fortress of the three pillar stones'.

SCATHACH

In Irish Celtic mythology, Scathach was a prophetess and great warrior. She is supposed to have run a kind of military school at which she passed on her skills in war to her pupils. The whereabouts of this school are unknown. It was not in Ireland, and it may have been somewhere in Scotland, such as the Isle of Skye, or even farther afield. One of her pupils was CUCHULAINN, to whom she is said to have given GAE-BHOLG, an invincible spear. While he was her pupil, which he was for a year and a day, he had an affair with her daughter, UATHACH. While Cuchulainn was studying war skills with Scathach, he fought AOIFE (2), the great rival of Scathach, in single combat and defeated her. He then became Aoife's lover and she bore him a son, CONNLAI.

SCENA *see* SKENA.

SCEOLAN *see* SGEOLAN.

SCEPTRE
Various archaeological excavations have revealed objects that appear to have been sceptres or maces. Frequently these have come to light at temple sites, and it is thought that they were part of the regalia of the priests. Some of these spectres or maces were quite plain but others were quite elaborate, with carvings relating to the cult of a particular divinity, such as the SUN-god.

SCORIATH *see* LABHRAIDH LOINGSECH.

SEACHRAN
In Irish Celtic mythology, Seachran was a giant who became a friend of FIONN MAN CUMHAILL. He took Fionn home to meet his family, but they were far from pleased that he had made friends with an ordinary mortal. During the feast given in honour of his guest, Seachran was seized by a great hairy

claw that seemed to come out of nowhere. In the course of trying to shake himself free from this horrible claw, he accidentally knocked his mother into a CAULDRON. In fact, the cauldron had been intended not for his mother, but for Seachran himself. Fearing for their safety, Fionn and Seachran fled. They were pursued by Seachran's brother, who killed Seachran but was in turn killed by Fionn. Fionn succeeded in bringing his friend back to life by using a magic ring.

SEANCHAN TORPEIST *see* IRUSAN.

SEARBHAN
In Irish Celtic mythology, Searbhan was a one-eyed GIANT who was sent to guard a magic rowan tree that had grown from a berry that had accidentally been let fall by one of the TUATHA DE DANANN. He was of a terrible appearance, and everyone was terrified of him, particularly as it was said that the only way that he could be killed was by three blows from his own iron club. He was eventually killed by DIARMAID ua Duibhne.

SEDANTA *see* SETANTA.

SEMION
In Irish Celtic mythology, Semion was the son of Stariat. The FIR BHOLG are said to have been descended from him.

SENACH
In Irish Celtic mythology, Senach was a warrior against whom CUCHULAINN did battle and won.

SENCHA

In Irish Celtic mythology, Sencha was the chief judge and poet of Ulster at the time of CONCHOBAR MAC NESSA.

SEQUENA

In Gaulish Celtic mythology, Sequena was the goddess of the source of the River Seine, which takes its name from her. A sanctuary to her was uncovered near the source and votive offerings found. She is said to have been associated with the duck.

SERA

In Irish Celtic mythology, Sera was the father of PARTHOLAN. According to some sources, it was not Partholan but Sera who was the husband of DEALGNAID.

SETANTA *or* SEDANTA

In Irish Celtic mythology, Setanta was the boyhood name of CUCHULAINN. While he still bore this name he performed his first noted heroic deed when he defeated all fifty youths who were in the service of CONCHOBAR MAC NESSA.

SGATHACH

In Irish Celtic mythology, Sgathach was the daughter of EANNA. FIONN MAC CUMHAILL, when at Eanna's home of Eanna, offered to marry Sgathach for a year and a day. Eanna and his wife agreed to this temporary marriage, but the girl was not in favour. While Fionn and his men were asleep, she played a tune on her magical harp, and next morning Fionn and his men found themselves far away from Eanna's home with no means of getting back there.

SGEIMH SOLAIS

In Irish Celtic mythology, Sgeimh Solais, whose name translates as 'light of beauty', was the daughter of CAIRBRE, a high king. A son of the king of the Desi tribe became betrothed to her. The betrothal led to the FIANNA asking Cairbre to pay a tribute. Cairbre's refusal led to the battle of GABHRA. This was to lead to the end of the supremacy of the Fianna in Ireland.

SGEOLAN *or* SCEOLAN

In Irish Celtic mythology, Sgeolan was one of the two faithful hounds of FIONN MAC CUMHAILL, the other one being BRAN (2). They were in fact the nephews as well as the hounds of Fionn. His sister, TUIREANN, who was married to ILLAN, was turned into a wolfhound by a druidess who was the mistress of her husband and who was jealous of Tuireann. Tuireann was pregnant when she was made to change shapes and gave birth when she was still in the form of a wolfhound.

SGILTI

In Welsh Celtic mythology, Sgilti was so light-footed that he could run across the ends of branches of trees. He was thus extremely useful when a swift runner was needed. Legend has it that he was one of the group of followers who were formed to help CULHWCH find OLWEN.

SHAPE-CHANGING

A very common motif in Celtic mythology and religion was shape-changing or shape-shifting, in line with Celtic belief that the soul is immortal. Divinities could turn themselves into the shape of their choice at will. For example, MORRIGAN and BADB frequently appeared in the form of crows or ravens to warriors in battle. Gods or people with supernatural powers could turn other people into other shapes, often animals, frequently as a punishment. TWRCH TRWYTH in Welsh mythology was turned into a boar from having been a king. Sometimes the act of shape-changing is the result of jealousy on the part of the person or god bringing about the metamorphosis. TUIREANN was turned into a wolfhound by the druid mistress of her husband Illan when she was pregnant because she was jealous of Tuireann, and the children of LIR were changed into swans by their stepmother because she was jealous of her father's love for them.

SIDENG

In Irish Celtic mythology, Sideng was the daughter of MONGAN. According to legend, she gave FIONN MAC CUMHAILL a flat stone to which a golden chain was attached. When Fionn whirled this stone round his head he was able to cut his opponents in half.

SIDH (*plural* SIDHE)

In Irish Celtic mythology, each member of the TUATHA DE DANANN was assigned part of the underground realm that was given to them when they were defeated by the Sons of MIL ESPAINE, and each part was called a *sidh*, the word meaning a mound or hill. Later the word was used not just to refer to the dwelling-place of a god but to a god himself, and thereafter by extension to a fairy, sprite or other supernatural being.

SILBURY HILL *see* HILL SITES.

SIMIAS

In Irish Celtic mythology, Simias was a wizard from the mythical city of MURIAS. He was one of the four wizards (the other three being ESIAS, MORFESSA and USCIAS) who taught the TUATHA DE DANANN their magic skills before they invaded Ireland. He is said to have given them the inexhaustible CAULDRON of the DAGHDA.

SINEND *see* LODAN.

SIONAN *or* SINAINN

In Irish Celtic mythology, Sionan was the daughter of LODAN, who was a son of LIR. She is associated with the River Shannon, which is said to be named after her. Legend has it that she went to a magical well underneath the sea. Sources vary as to whether she had been forbidden to do so or whether she omitted to cast a certain spell, but, in any event, she incurred the wrath of the spirit of the well. The WATER from the well rose up and chased her westward to the west coast of Ireland where she drowned, becoming the source of the Shannon.

SINIANN *see* SIONAN.

SIRONA

In Gaulish Celtic mythology, Sirona was a goddess whose name means 'star', although there is no evidence that she played any kind of celestial part in Celtic belief. She was particularly associated with healing shrines and was often depicted in association with GRANNOS, who may have been assimilated with the classical god Apollo. Although Sirona was depicted as the consort of Grannos or Apollo, she is thought to have existed as an independent divinity before the Romano-Celtic period. She was associated with regeneration and fertility as well as with healing.

SIUGMALL
In Irish Celtic mythology, Siugmall was the grandson of MIDHIR and FUAMNACH. One legend has it that he helped his grandmother to dispose of Edain Echraidhe, and as a result was killed with her.

SKENA *or* SCENA
In Irish Celtic mythology, Skena was the wife of AMHAIRGHIN, one of the Sons of MIL ESPAINE. She died on the voyage to Ireland and was buried when the expedition arrived in Ireland.

SKY
In Celtic mythology and belief, sky deities appear to have existed separately from SUN deities, the sky god having ascendancy over all the elements associated with the sky and being a champion of light and life as opposed to the forces of darkness and death. The classical sky god Jupiter was assimilated into the Celtic range of deities.

SMIRGAT
In Irish Celtic mythology, Smirgat, according to some sources, was the wife of FIONN MAC CUMHAILL towards the end of his life. She is said to have prophesied that he would die if he should ever drink from a horn. For that reason he was always extremely careful always to drink from a cup, goblet or bowl.

SMITH

The art of the smith was of importance to the Celts, not least because they forged the weapons so essential to an essentially warlike people. The art of taking a lump of stone or ore and fashioning into something essential to war, such as a spear, was held in such high regard that smiths were sometimes credited with supernatural powers. There is some archaeological evidence pointing to a kind of smith cult. Particularly in northern parts of Britain, such as Durham and Yorkshire, there have been uncovered potsherds that are decorated with the tools associated with smiths. In addition, a bronze image of a smith was discovered at Sunderland, and a site in Northumberland produced a complete figure of a smith god applied to a vessel made of pottery. He is depicted as standing over an anvil with, in one hand, an ingot held in a pair of tongs and in the other hand a hammer, the tools of his trade. The shard of pottery depicting this is thought to date from around the second century AD. There are various examples of divine smiths in Celtic mythology. In Irish legend, GOIBHNIU, for example, fashioned magical weapons for the other gods.

SNAKE

In Celtic mythology and belief, the snake was associated with fertility and with healing and also with the Otherworld. SIRONA, for example, a Gaulish goddess associated with healing, is depicted with a serpent twined round her arm. Because of the rippling movement of the snake, it is often associated with water. In one of the tales of the hero FIONN MAC CUMHAILL, he is recorded as being skilled at killing water snakes. There are various tales relating to snakes or serpents in Celtic mythology. A famous one relates to MEICHE, the son of MORRIGAN. It was prophesied that he would bring great disaster to Ireland. He was born with three hearts, one for each manifestation of his mother, and each of these hearts contained a serpent. These were revealed when he was killed and cut open by DIAN CECHT. Two of them were burnt, but one legend has it that the third escaped and grew into a huge serpent that was later killed by Dian Cecht. Thus the prophesy of wholesale disaster for Ireland was averted.

SOL

In Welsh Celtic mythology, Sol was one of the members of the group that was formed to help CULHWCH in his quest for OLWEN. He was selected to be part of the group because he could stand on one foot all day.

SONS OF MIL ESPAINE *see* MIL ESPAINE, SONS OF.

SOUTH CADBURY CASTLE

There are the remains of an Iron Age fortified town at South Cadbury in Somerset. It appears to have been a centre of Celtic religious activity, and of particular interest is the body of a young man, which was buried in the rear of the bank. This seems to have been interred either as a token of good luck or as an act of propitiation to the gods, but it is not clear whether his death was accidental or whether it was an act of human SACRIFICE. Whether or not the Celts engaged in human sacrifice is the subject of dispute, and the young man might simply have died in battle or as a result of natural causes. On the other hand, the site was found to contain evidence of animal sacrifice, with the remains of young domestic animals such as piglets, calves and lambs.

SPIRIT OF IRELAND

The actual identity of the 'Spirit of Ireland', also known as the 'Sovereignty of Ireland' or 'the Sovranty of Ireland', is subject to uncertainty and confusion. That this being was female in form and that she embodied the very essence of Ireland is not in doubt. As such, she was one of the most important Irish deities. The ritual surrounding her is also a bit shadowy, but she is held to have had the right to confer the status of king and to have a ritual mating with the successful candidate. Some sources indicate that the spirit of Ireland was personified as MEDB, and others that she was the personification of the most beautiful woman in Ireland, such as Edain Echraidhe (*see* HORSES). Another source has it that the spirit of Ireland was Banbha (*see* ERIU).

SPRINGS

WATER was generally important to the Celts, but of special importance to them were springs, which were considered to have healing powers. Because springs by their very nature well up from below the ground, they were often credited with supernatural associations, as though they provided a link between the mortal world and the OTHERWORLD. During the Romano-Celtic period the concept of the healing spring was developed to an even greater extent. At that point the Celtic goddess SIRONA, who was associated with healing, became known also as a consort of the classical god Apollo. One of

211

the interesting features of the healing springs of the Romano-Celtic period was the presentation of model votive offerings of the part of the body that was suffering from disease. Thus, if the model of a diseased arm was presented as a votive offering to the god or goddess who was the spirit of the spring, the hope was that the arm would become whole.

SRENG

In Irish Celtic mythology, Sreng was a FIR BHOLG warrior who was despatched as an ambassador to have talks with the TUATHA DE DANANN when they landed with their invading force in Ireland. He spoke to BRES, who was put forward as the spokesman of the Tuatha De Danann and who suggested that the land of Ireland should be divided between the Fir Bholgs and the Tuatha De Danann. The Fir Bholg rejected this suggestion, and this led to the first Battle of MAGH TUIREDH. Although the Fir Bholgs gained some initial success when Sreng and NUADA fought in single combat and Sreng succeeded in severing Nuada's arm, the Fir Bholgs were eventually soundly defeated.

STAG

The stag was important in Celtic mythology and beliefs. The stag was a symbol of virility, dignity, speed and aggression. It also had additional associations. The antlers of the stag were symbolic of the branches of a tree, and TREES were sacred to the Celts. The shedding of their antlers, in common with the shedding of their leaves by trees, was a symbol of regeneration. The Celtic god who was most closely linked with stags is CERNUNNOS. He wore antlers on his head and was often depicted as being accompanied with a stag or stags. Stags and deer play a significant part in Celtic mythology, as is evident in the legend of PWYLL's encounter with ARAWN, when he chased away Arawn's hounds, which were in pursuit of a stag, and in penance had to change forms and countries with Arawn for a year. *See also* WHITE STAG.

STARIAT *see* SEMION.

STARN
In Irish Celtic mythology, Starn was a son of SERA and brother of PARTHOLAN.

STONEHENGE
According to Celtic mythology, MYRDDIN is said to have had Stonehenge built with stones brought from Ireland. In Ireland, they had formed the GIANTS' RING on Mount KILLARAUS. According to legend, the stones had been carried by GIANTS who originated in Africa and who were the first inhabitants of the earth.

STRETTWEG
At Strettweg in Austria was discovered a unique bronze wagon model. It is thought to date from the seventh century BC and thus belongs to the early Celtic period or HALLSTATT CULTURE. The model comprises a platform on four wheels, at each end of which is an image of a STAG with antlers. In the centre stands a woman carrying a flat bowl on her head, and she is surrounded by a group of cavalrymen and infantrymen with spears and shields. It is thought that this might represent a ritual hunt.

SUALTAM

In Irish Celtic mythology, Sualtam was the mortal father of CUCHULAINN. The night before his wedding to DEICHTIRE, the god LUGH carried her off and slept with her, and SETANTA (CUCHULAINN) was later born. When MEDB invaded Ulster in quest of the great brown bull of Ulster, Sualtam tried to rouse the men of Ulster to action. He then turned his horse, the Grey of Macha, so angrily and suddenly that the sharp rim of his shield cut off his head. The severed head then continued to call out a warning to the men of Ulster until the curse that Macha had placed on them was lifted and they were once again men of action.

SUANTRADE

In Irish Celtic mythology, Suantrade was one of the harpists of UAITHNE who made such sad music that men died while listening.

SUCCAT

Either the childhood name or the nickname of St PATRICK was Succat.

SUCELLUS

In Gaulish Celtic mythology, Sucellus, which translates as 'good striker', was a god who is often depicted as carrying a long-handled mallet, has a wine cask or drinking vessel near, and is often accompanied by a dog.

SULIS

The name of the goddess who presided over the healing SPRING at Bath was Sulis. When the Romans came to Britain they converted the healing springs at Bath into a large bath house and built a temple, but the site of the springs is thought to have been sacred to healing long before their arrival. Sulis was one of the British Celtic WATER deities and, as befits her association with Bath, was a goddess of healing. The Romans held Sulis in such regard that they named the town that is now Bath after her, the Roman name for it being Aquae Sulis. From the time of the arrival of the Romans, Sulis began to be identified with the classical goddess Minerva. This hybridization of Celtic and Roman deities was quite common, and the hybridized goddess became known as Sulis Minerva. She was the presiding goddess of the therapeutic springs at Bath in Roman times.

SUN

That the Celts venerated the sun is obvious from the motifs on various artefacts that have come to light during archaeological expeditions. Particularly common are depictions of the WHEEL as a solar symbol. Although it is to be expected that the Celts would be sun-worshippers since they venerated natural phenomena generally, such as WATER and TREES, there is little evidence of sun-gods in Celtic literature. The Irish god LUGH, whose name means 'shining one', who had a beautiful, radiant countenance and was associated with light, is an obvious candidate to have been a sun-god. The Gaulish god BELENUS was also associated with light, the word *bel* being translated as 'bright', but he was known as a god of light and healing rather than specifically as a sun-god.

SUN-GOD *see* SUN.

SWAN

In Celtic mythology and beliefs, the swan was of particular importance. In HALLSTATT Europe archaeologists have uncovered model wagons, drawn by creatures resembling swans, the wagons sometimes carrying vessels. Swans were common in Celtic legend and seem to have been a favourite in SHAPE-CHANGING. The children of LIR were turned into swans by their stepmother because she was jealous of their father's love for them. In another legend, MIDHIR changes himself and ETAIN into swans to escape from the court of EOCHAIDH. In yet another, CAER, who was beloved by OENGHUS, became a swan every other year and Oenghus turned into a swan to fly away with her.

SWASTIKA

In Celtic Europe, the swastika was a solar motif in the way that the WHEEL was. Swastikas have been found on stone altars and as a motif on artefacts. Sometimes it appears alone and sometimes accompanied by a wheel motif. It is thought that perhaps it was indicative of good luck as well as being a solar motif.

T

TAILTINN

In Irish Celtic mythology, the battle at which the Sons of MIL ESPAINE defeated the TUATHA DE DANANN for the second time was the Battle of Tailtinn. After it, MAC CECHT, MAC CUILL and MAC GREINE became rulers of Ireland and the Tuatha De Danann were given the underground portion of the country.

TAIN BO CUAILNGE

The basis of the Tain Bo Cuailnge is the quest of MEDB, queen of Connacht, for the DONN CUAILNGE, the great brown bull of Ulster, partly because her husband, AILILL, owned FINNBHENACH, the white-horned bull of Connacht. Ulster was the traditional enemy of Medb's kingdom, and so in order to acquire the bull that she so much desired she had to raise an army with which to invade Ulster. At that time the warriors of Ulster were unfit for battle since MACHA had placed a curse on them, and the only warrior who was fit to fight was CUCHULAINN. He put up a spirited defence against Medb, single-handedly holding off her troops for many weeks. Eventually he was killed and the bull captured and taken to Medb's camp where it had an epic fight lasting a day and night with Finnbhenach, and the white-horned bull was killed and torn to pieces. Later, Donn Cuailnge returned to Ulster where it died.

TALIESIN

In Welsh Celtic mythology, Taliesin was the son of CERRIDWEN, and he was born under strange, supernatural circumstances. Cerridwen had two, or perhaps three, children born before the birth of Taliesin. Of these, one was Crearwy, an extremely beautiful daughter, and one was Afagddu, a very ugly son. To compensate her son for his unfortunate physical appearance, Cerridwen decided to try to endow him with other virtues, specifically special powers relating to inspiration and knowledge. To do this, she brewed a potion of various herbs in a large CAULDRON, the contents of which had to boil for a year and a day in order to have the required result, which was three drops of magical fluid that would endow Afagddu with the desired talents. GWION BACH was appointed to stir the potion regularly, and towards the end of the year he accidentally splashed his finger with three drops of the potion from the cauldron. Without thinking, he put his fingers in his mouth to cool them and so partook of the magical brew. Fearing for his life, he fled, and the cauldron, having been deprived of its three magical drops of fluid, cracked, the remainder of the potion running into a stream. Cerridwen set off in pursuit of Gwion, he frequently changing shape to avoid her and she frequently changing shape in order to catch him. After a great deal of SHAPE-CHANGING, Gwion changed himself into a grain of wheat on the threshing floor of a barn and was eaten by Cerridwen, who had turned into a hen. Having swallowed the grain of wheat, Cerridwen discovered that she was pregnant and gave birth to a beautiful baby boy. She did not want the child but was unwilling to kill him. She therefore put the child in a bag and threw him into the river. The bag and child were retrieved by ELFFIN, who is said to have been so impressed by the beauty of the baby's brow that he called out 'Taliesin', meaning 'radiant brow', and so the child was named. Taliesin inherited the inspirational powers originally intended for Afagddu and became famous for his poetic prowess and was also said to have had the gift of prophecy. He is said to have become a bard at the court of King ARTHUR.

Taliesin is thought not only to have been a legendary figure but also to have been a historical figure, noted for his poetic powers.

TARA

For many centuries the most sacred place in Ireland, and the main residence of the high kings, was Tara in County Meath, the ancient site dating back to 2000 BC. It was regarded as the Celtic capital of Ireland, being an important religious and political centre, although the site of Tara is thought to have been a sacred one long before the Celts, possibly from Neolithic times. Tara features in various Irish Celtic legends. It was the capital of the TUATHA DE DANANN and the location of the court of CONCHOBAR MAC NESSA and thus the home of the RED BRANCH.

TARANIS

The Celts believed that the weather was a manifestation of the supernatural powers of their gods, and several of their divinities were personifications of natural phenomena. Thunder and storms with their noise and turbulence may have indicated a power struggle among the gods. Taranis was their thunder god. The Roman poet Lucan, who lived around the first century AD, wrote about events that occurred around the middle of the first century BC, mainly an account of the civil war between Pompey and Caesar in his poem *The Pharsalia*. He referred to a Celtic god called Taranis and described the cult surrounding the god as being very cruel. Taranis has also been equated with the Roman god Jupiter, who was often depicted brandishing a thunderbolt and has been associated with war as well as thunder. Although it has been assumed that Lucan considered Taranis to be quite an important god, only seven altars dedicated to him have been found. On the other hand, these altars are widely spread, from Britain to Gaul to Germany to Dalmatia, there being one at Chester in Britain.

TARBHFEIS

In Irish Celtic mythology, Tarbhfeis, which survives in various spellings and is translated as 'the bull feast', was a ceremony associated with the selection of the high kings of Ireland. The ceremony was held at TARA and was conducted by five DRUIDS. One of them had to eat the flesh of a bull and drink its blood before being put to sleep by the other four druids as they chanted over him. He would then have a dream about the person who was chosen to become high king. Obviously, he could lie, but he was under threat of being destroyed by the gods if he did not tell the truth. The rite is said to have been outlawed by St PATRICK.

TECH DUINN

In Irish Celtic mythology, Tech Duinn is said to have been the name given to an island off the southwest coast of Ireland. It was believed to be the home of DONN, the god of the dead. One legend has it that he was the son of Midhir the Proud, but another identifies him with Donn, one of the Sons of MIL ESPAINE, who drowned on the voyage of the Sons and was buried on the island.

TETHRA see OGHMA.

TEUTATES

One of the Celtic gods was Teutates, said to have been a Gaulish tribal deity. He is described as being connected with arts, journeys and trading.

TEYRNON

In Irish Celtic mythology, Teyrnon was the lord of Gwent Is-Coed. He is best known as the foster father of PRYDERI, whom he found on his doorstep as a baby. He named the baby boy GWRI, and looked after him until he was struck by the child's resemblance to PWYLL. He then told Pwyll that his son was still alive.

TIGERNMAS

In Irish Celtic mythology, Tigernmas was a king who may have had some historical connections. Said to have been the son of Follach, he supposedly introduced the worship of Cenn Cruiach to Ireland. This worship involved human sacrifice on the feast of SAMHAIN. He and many of his followers are said to have been slain at one of these ritual feasts. Some

sources indicate that he was credited with introducing min-
ing and the smelting of gold into Ireland.

TIR NA MBAN

In Irish Celtic mythology, Tir na mBan was an OTHERWORLD
country, an island that was populated entirely by women. It is
said to have been visited by BRAN (1) and his followers, who
thought that they had left after a year but had in fact stayed
for several hundred years.

TIR NA OG or TIR NA NOG

In Irish Celtic mythology, Tir na Og, which has various spell-
ing variants, was an OTHERWORLD realm in which people are
forever young. It is thus sometimes known as the 'land of the
forever young' or the 'land of youth'.

TIR TAIRNIGIRIB see MANANNAN MAC LIR.

TOLLUND MAN

In 1950, the body of a man, known as Tollund Man, was
discovered in a peat bog in Denmark. He had been garrotted and was wearing only a leather cap and girdle, bearing
a marked resemblance to the state of LINDOW MAN. He is
thought to have been placed in the bog around 500 BC and
may have been deposited there by a Teutonic tribe rather
than a Celtic tribe, since some of the Teutonic tribes are
thought to have shared some traditions and customs with
the Celts.

TOPA

In Irish Celtic mythology, Topa was a manservant of

PARTHOLAN who was seduced by the wife of Partholan and so who may have been the father of RURY.

TORACH *see* TORY ISLAND.

TORC
The Celtic neck-ring was known as a torc. Torcs were often found round the necks of Celtic deities. CERNUNNOS, the STAG-antlered god, is depicted on the GUNDESTRUP CAULDRON as wearing one torc round his neck and carrying another in his hand. The same god has also been depicted with a torc hung over each antler. When worn by mortals, they were often a sign of nobility or high status. For example, the prince who was buried at HALLSTATT was interred wearing a torc. Torcs were often made of gold and could be extremely heavy.

TORC TRIATH
In Irish Celtic mythology, Torc Triath was the king of the BOARS. It is said to have been the Irish equivalent of TWRCH TRWYTH, against which CULHWCH was sent by YSPADDADEN as one of the tasks set to win the hand of OLWEN.

TORS *see* HILL SITES.

TORY ISLAND
In Irish Celtic mythology, the FOMORII had a stronghold on Tory Island. The name derives from the word *torach*, meaning a watchtower, and the island is sometimes referred to as Torach.

TREES
The Celts held trees to be sacred, both as individual species,

such as the OAK, and as collections of trees, such as woods and groves. Trees were thought by the Celts to represent a link between the upper or mortal world and the OTHERWORLD or lower world, the roots spreading deep into the ground and the branches reaching high into the sky. Trees were also thought of as representing the Tree of Life, and as such were regarded as being associated with fertility. The falling of the leaves of deciduous trees in the autumn and the appearance of buds and young leaves was also thought to be related to the Celts' philosophy of regeneration.

TRI DE DANA
In Irish Celtic mythology, the Tri De Dana was the triad of gods associated with craftsmanship. They were Creidhne, GOIBHNIU and LUCHTA. They forged and repaired the magical weapons of the TUATHA DE DANANN.

TRINOVANTES
This was the tribal name given to the Britons who were said to be inhabiting London, and the territory to the north of there, at the time of the second invasion of Julius Caesar in 54 BC.

TRIPLISM
The NUMBER three played an important part in Celtic culture and beliefs. Triads were common, and the concept of the triple goddess was particularly common. For example, MORRIGAN was a triple war goddess, as was MACHA.

TUACHELL *see* NECHTA SCENE.

TUAN MAC CARELL

In Irish Celtic mythology, Tuan mac Carell is said to have been the son of Starn, brother of PARTHOLAN. He is supposed to have survived a plague that destroyed most other people and to have been reborn as a STAG. He was then reborn as an eagle and again as a salmon. When in the form of a salmon, he was eaten by his wife. She then gave birth to him in human form. Another legend has it that Tuan mac Carell was a reincarnation of Tuan mac Stern, who was the nephew of Partholan.

TUAN MAC STERN *see* PARTHOLAN; TUAN MAC CARELL.

TUATHA DE DANANN

In Irish Celtic mythology, the gods of pre-Christian Ireland were known as the Tuatha De Danann, which translates as the 'people of the goddess DANU'. When the Tuatha De Danann arrived in Ireland, they fought two great battles, the first against the previous invaders, the FIR BHOLG, and the second against the FOMORII. The Tuatha De Danann defeated the Fir Bholg at the first Battle of MAGH TUIREDH. The defeat meant that the Fir Bholg had to hand over the kingship of Ireland to the Tuatha, but the king of the Tuatha, NUADA, lost an arm in the battle and so was forced to abdicate. In his place, BRES was chosen to be leader and king, but his leadership was not a success and Nuada, having had an artificial silver arm fitted, was restored to the throne. Bres then defected to the Fomorii and raised an army against the Tuatha. LUGH became the leader of the Tuatha, Nuada having stepped down in his favour.

The second Battle of Magh Tuiredh was then fought between the Tuatha under Lugh and the Fomorii under Bres. This battle was to be decided on the result of single combat between Lugh and the giant BALOR. Lugh won when he delivered a slingshot that went right through Balor's single eye and out of the back of his head to kill or injure some of the Fomorii followers.

The Tuatha were finally defeated by the invasionary force of the Sons of MIL ESPAINE, and the Tuatha were given the underground part of Ireland for their realm.

TUIREANN (1)

In Irish Celtic mythology, Tuireann is rather a shadowy figure or figures. The name is given in one legend to the wife of ILLAN. When she was pregnant, she was turned into a wolfhound by her husband's mistress. Instead of giving birth to children, Tuireann gave birth to two wolfhounds, BRAN (2) and SGEOLAN, who became the faithful hunting hounds of FIONN MAC CUMHAILL, the brother-in-law of Tuireann. She was returned to human form after Illan had promised his mistress that he would renounce her.

TUIREANN (2) *see* TUIRENN.

TUIRENN *or* TUIREANN

In Irish Celtic mythology, Tuirenn was the father of Brian, IUCHAR and Iucharba, possibly by the goddess BRIGID.

TWRCH TRWYTH

In Welsh Celtic mythology, Twrch Trwyth was a fierce BOAR

who had been a king before being transformed. In Irish Celtic mythology, TORC TRIATH was his equivalent. In the legend of CULHWCH and OLWEN, one of the tasks that Culhwch had to perform to win her hand was to obtain the comb and razor, or the comb, razor and shears, that lay between the ears of the beast so that he could act as barber to YSPADDADEN. With some help, he accomplished the task and the boar was forced to jump off a cliff into the sea.

TYLWYTH TEG
In Welsh Celtic mythology, Tylwyth Teg was the collective name given to the people of GWYN AP NUDD. The name probably referred to spirits who were waiting to be born again rather than the dead, and so can perhaps can be regarded more as a type of fairies.

U

UAITHNE

In Irish Celtic mythology, Uaithne was the harp of the DAGHDA. It was a magic instrument and would play only when it was asked to do so by one of the Daghda. The instrument was stolen by the FOMORII, but the Daghda discovered the theft and traced it to the feasting hall of their enemy. They then called to the instrument and it leapt forward, killing nine Fomorii in the process, and began to play a song of praise to the Daghda.

Uaithne was also the name of the Daghda's harpist. He is said to have had an affair with BOANN, the water-goddess, who bore him three sons who played such sad music that men were said to have died of sorrow when listening to it.

UATHACH

In Irish Celtic mythology, Uathach was the daughter of SCATHACH, a female prophet and warrior who took pupils to train them in the martial arts at her home in Alba. One of these pupils was CUCHULAINN. Legend has it that after his arrival at Scathach's fortress he was offered some refreshment by Uathach. When she was serving it to him, he forgot how strong he was and broke her finger as she passed him some food. She screamed aloud in pain, and her lover, Cochar Crufe, came to see what was the matter. He challenged Cuchulainn to single combat and was slain. Uathach became Cuchulainn's mistress and perhaps his wife.

UATH MAC IMOMAN

In Irish Celtic mythology, Uath is said to have been able to turn himself into any shape. He was asked to decide whether CUCHULAINN, LAOGHAIRE or CONALL was the greatest warrior in the whole of Ireland. In order to come to a decision, he asked them to cut off his head and come back the next day so that he could cut off each of theirs. There are two different versions of the legend from then on. In one, Laoghaire and Conall refused to accede to Uath's request because they feared that they, unlike Uath, would not have the powers to stay alive if they had been decapitated. In another version, Laoghaire and Conall agreed to cut off Uath's head but did not return the next day to have theirs cut off. Cuchulainn agrees to the request in both versions of the legend. He cut off Uath's head, but when Uath came to cut off Cuchulainn's head, the blade of the axe reversed and spared him. Uath then hailed him as the champion warrior, although his two rivals refused to accept the decision. There are various other legends describing how the contest for greatest Irish warrior was decided.

UGAINE MOR

In Irish Celtic mythology, Ugaine Mor was a high king in the sixth century BC, although he may be partly historical. He is supposed to have ruled the whole of Ireland and part of Western Europe, particularly GAUL. He married a Gaulish princess and their children included Laoghaire Lorc and Cobthach, who fought over the right to succeed their father as high king. On Ugaine's death, Ireland was divided into twenty-five parts among his children, and this system lasted for three hundred years.

UIGREANN
In Irish Celtic mythology, Uigreann fought Cumhaill, the father of FIONN MAC CUMHAILL because of Cumhaill's abduction of Muirne. He was later killed by Cumhaill, and his sons are said to have sought vengeance for their father's death. According to some sources, each of the sons threw a spear at Cumhaill and all five were credited with killing their father's killer.

UI NEILL *see* NIALL.

UISNECH *see* NAOISE.

ULAID
The original Irish name for Ulster was Ulaid. It appears to have covered approximately the geographical area of the modern province. Its capital was EMHAIN MACHA.

ULLAN *see* ILLAN.

ULSTER
In Irish Celtic mythology, Ulster was one of the five provinces into which the Fir Bholg divided Ireland. It was the great enemy and rival of CONNACHT (*see also* TAIN BO

CUAILGNE). Ulster had several heroes associated with it, principally CUCHULAINN.

UNDRY
In Irish Celtic mythology, the magic CAULDRON of the DAGHDA was called Undry. It had an unlimited supply of food that was never used up, no matter how many people ate from it. No worthy person ever went away hungry from it and everyone got food from it in proportion to their merits.

UNIUS
In Irish Celtic mythology, Unius was the name of the river over which MORRIGAN stood with one foot on each bank when she was making love to the DAGHDA.

URIEN
Urien was an historical sixth-century AD king of Rheged who defeated the Anglo-Saxons at Argoed Llwyfain. He is said to have been the father of OWAIN. He was assassinated.

USCIAS
In Irish Celtic mythology, Uscias was one of the four wizards who taught their magic to the TUATHA DE DANANN before they came to Ireland, the others being ESIAS, MORFESSA and Simias.

V

VIX

A Celtic princess was buried in a barrow at Vix in Burgundy in France in the sixth century BC. Known as the Princess of Vix, her grave with its grave goods, which was excavated in 1953, significantly added to our knowledge of the Celts. The body of the princess was laid on a four-wheeled wagon that was adorned with gold, brooches and amber jewellery. It also contained a very large, very heavy Grecian vase. Various other valuable artefacts were buried with the princess. The lavishness of the grave goods for her journey to the OTHERWORLD points to the fact that women in Celtic culture could achieve high rank and importance, and their nature also points to the fact that the early Celts traded with the Greeks, the Etruscans and with Rome and Burgundy.

VORTIGERN

This name means 'overlord' and may have been a title rather than a name. He is generally thought of as being a historical figure, although, as is frequently the case with Celtic historical figures, facts and legends have become somewhat jumbled. He is said to have been ruler of Britain in the fifth century AD and to have married a daughter of the rebel Roman emperor Maximus. He is mentioned by GEOFFREY OF MONMOUTH. Vortigern is said to have instigated the assassination of Constantine, king of Britain, by a Pict and to have installed Constantine's son, Constans, as a puppet king. Later he is said to have killed Constans in order to get the throne for himself. He is also said to have invited Saxons to Britain in order to rid the kingdom of the PICTS, but they began to carve out territory for themselves. Vortigern is said to have fled to Wales after the murder of some British princes on Salisbury Plain. While in Wales he tried to build a tower, only to find that the stones that had been built up during the day disappeared during the night. MYRDDIN ascribed the disappearance of the stones to a dragon. The king is said to have been burned to death in his tower, which was finally built by Ambrosius Aurelius, the rightful heir to the throne.

W

WANBOROUGH

This is the site of a Romano-Celtic temple in Surrey. The presence of three bronze chain headdresses indicates the sacred nature of the site in Celtic times, since such headdresses were worn by priests who were officiating at religious ceremonies in temples. The miniature bronze WHEELS that surmounted two of the headdresses suggest that they would have been worn by priests who were associated with the worship of the SUN. Significant quantities of Celtic coins uncovered underneath the level at which Roman remains were found suggest that the site was sacred to the Celts before the advent of the Romans.

WAR

The Celts were a warlike people. This is obvious from the archaeological evidence that has been retrieved from various excavations. Shields, spears, etc, were a common part of the grave goods interred with the corpse to help the soul in its journey to, and life in, the OTHERWORLD. It is also evident from the votive offerings to gods that have been uncovered from LAKES, rivers, pools and BOGS. These were not necessarily intended for war-gods but were perhaps to be regarded as offerings to the god or spirit of the piece of water concerned. Many of the weapons so presented had been deliberately broken or damaged before being offered, perhaps because the Celts felt that such weapons had to be rendered unfit for use in this world before they would be acceptable to the god (*see* RITUAL DAMAGE). Miniature weapons were also often offered as gifts to the gods in shrines.

Images of warriors and of war-gods were a common part of the Celtic culture. Life-size sculptures of war-gods clad in full armour have been discovered in various shrines, and many Celtic coins depict male and female warriors. In the north of Britain some of the representations of war-gods not only bear shields and spears to exhibit their warlike connections, but they were also depicted wearing HORNS, sometimes RAM horns, which suggested not only aggression but sexual aggression. This was further emphasized by the fact that such depictions of war-gods were often naked and had exaggeratedly large phalluses. In Irish Celtic mythology, several of the war-deities were female, such as MACHA and MORRIGAN. Here again, the warlike qualities of the goddesses were often accompanied by attributes of sexuality and fertility.

WATER

The Celts appear to have venerated water, seeing it not only as essential to life but perhaps seeing it as having connections with the OTHERWORLD. This would obviously be more true of forms of water that came from deep down within the earth, such as WELLS and springs. That water was venerated is obvious from the quantities of weapons and valuable artefacts, such as items of jewellery, coins, items of domestic life, such as CAULDRONS, and even animal and human SACRIFICES, that have been retrieved from RIVERS, SPRINGS, LAKES, pools and WELLS. Rivers, lakes and so on were thought to have spirits or gods associated with them who would appreciate such votive offerings—some of them were shrines.

Water in Celtic times, as later, was thought to be a source of healing. Especially during the late pre-Roman Celtic period and the Romano-Celtic period, healing shrines grew up around natural springs that were thought to have healing powers. This association with water and natural healing powers lasted far longer than Celtic society—one has only to think of Bath and its associations with healing.

WELLS

As has been pointed out at WATER, wells, in common with rivers, springs, lakes and pools, were venerated by the Celts. Wells were especially venerated, partly because of their supposed healing properties but also because they were perceived as forming a connection between the mortal world and the OTHERWORLD.

WHEEL

In the Romano-Celtic period, the wheel was regarded as being a symbol of the SUN, probably because the wheel, being circular, bears a resemblance to the sun with spokes radiating out from it. The Celts sometimes buried model wheels with corpses, perhaps as symbols of the sun to light the way of the dead to the OTHERWORLD.

WHITE MOUNT

In British Celtic mythology, the head of BENDIGEID VRAN was buried by MANAWYDAN FAB LLYR, PRYDERI and others in the White Mount, one of the major druidic sites in London. The supposed founder of London, BRUTUS, was also buried there. It is said that King ARTHUR dug up the interred head of Bran so that he himself would be the only guardian of Britain, a role to which Bran had laid claim. With this in mind, he had ordered his head to be buried facing towards France, a potential enemy of Britain.

WHITE STAG

To the Celts the white STAG was a mystical animal thought to have come from the OTHERWORLD originally and so was endowed with special powers. The animal features in several Celtic legends.

WRNACH

In Welsh Celtic mythology, Wrnach was a GIANT who owned a sword that CULHWCH had to get hold of somehow as one of the tasks imposed on him by YSPADDADEN. CET obtained the sword by trickery and killed Wrnach.

Y

YNAWAG
In Welsh Celtic mythology, Ynawag was one of the seven survivors of the expedition led by BENDIGEID VRAN or Bran the Blessed against MATHOLWCH, then king of Ireland, to rescue BRANWEN. He was thus part of the group who carried the head of Bendigeid to be buried under the WHITE MOUNT in London.

YNYS WITTRIN *see* GLASTONBURY TOR.

YSPADDADEN
In Welsh Celtic mythology, Yspaddaden, whose name meant 'chief giant', according to legend had such huge, heavy eyelids that they had to be propped open by metal supports before he could see anything. He was the father of OLWEN, whom CULHWCH wanted to marry. The stepmother of Culhwch was so angry with him for refusing to marry her daughter that she pronounced a curse on him by which the only woman he could marry was the daughter of the notorious giant of Pencawr, Yspaddaden. Culhwch gathered together a group of companions and set out for the fortress of the giant. When the giant was asked to agree to the marriage of Olwen and Culhwch, he told Culhwch that he would give them his answer the next

day and that they should return to the fortress then. However, it was clear that he did not want to give the marriage his blessing when he threw a large, poisoned spear at them as they left the fortress. Bedwyr, one of Culhwch's companions, caught the spear and threw it back at the giant, wounding him in the knee. This episode is said to have been repeated on each of the next three days, Yspaddaden being wounded in the chest and in the eye. The giant then agreed to the marriage but imposed a number of seemingly impossible tasks, usually said to be thirteen in number, with various subsidiary tasks. With the help of various forms of supernatural powers and with the assistance of various people, Culhwch succeeded in his attempts to perform the tasks, but the giant kept changing the rules and conditions. Finally, Culhwch could take no more, and he and some companions stormed the giant's fortress. Yspaddaden was killed.

YWERIT

According to some sources of Welsh Celtic mythology, Ywerit was the father of BENDIGEID VRAN or Bran the Blessed.